Greetings from MAINE

Recipes *from the* Maine Kitchen

Cancer Community Center

Greetings from Maine...

The Cancer Community Center opened its doors in 1998. Located in South Portland, Maine, we are an independent agency providing peer-based support and wellness activities for adults who have been diagnosed with cancer. Staying true to the vision of our founder, Jane Staley, the Center strives daily to improve the quality of their lives by providing programs that enhance and complement traditional medical care. The center also recognizes that families and friends are impacted by this diagnosis, so make all programs available to them as well. Programs and activities include a wellness program, a one-to-one support program known as the Maine Buddy Program™, group support services, a resource library, informational sessions, on-site support for employees in the workplace, and a creative expression program.

All activities at the Center are made possible by the generosity of the community and are offered at no charge to participants. The entire annual budget must be raised within the community each year. The net proceeds of the sales of this cookbook will go directly to support the programs of the Center.

Additional copies of "Greetings from Maine" may be obtained online at www.cancercommunitycenter.org, or submit the order form at the end of this book.

For more information please contact:
Cancer Community Center
778 Maine Street
South Portland, Maine 04097
(207) 774-2200
(877) 774-2200
www.cancercommunitycenter.org

This cookbook is a collection of favorite recipes, which are not necessarily original recipes.

WIMMER
COOKBOOKS

A CONSOLIDATED GRAPHICS COMPANY

800.548.2537 wimmerco.com

Greetings from Maine... "the way life should be." Maine, or "Vacationland" as our license plate boasts, is indeed a special and enchanting place. Almost the size of the rest of the New England states put together, Maine offers 17 million acres of forests, beautiful mountains topped by mile-high Mount Katahdin, and 6,000 lakes and ponds. The state's magnificent 3,500 mile coastline is home to 60 lighthouses and over 2,000 islands. Gastronomically speaking, Maine is especially known for its wild blueberries and delicious fresh seafood.

Friends of the Cancer Community Center have gathered this collection of our favorite recipes to share a little part of our beautiful state with you. These recipes became our favorites because they fit so well with our Maine lifestyle. With the great outdoors beckoning us from our kitchens on a year-round basis, recipes have to be simple and easy. And since we often find ourselves sharing our beloved state with visitors, cooking for a crowd is a requirement. We hope you enjoy these recipes as much as we do and that they remind you of your love for the great state of Maine. Whether you're a Mainer yourself, or love to visit us, or are still dreaming about your first time "downeast," this cookbook will be a welcome addition to your kitchen.

Fran Philip
Editor, *Greetings from Maine*

This cookbook was the effort of many, including the recipe contributors and testers who are listed alphabetically at the end of the book. We would like to extend special thanks to the following people:

STEERING COMMITTEE

Fran Philip, Editor
Cherrie Cianchette, Section Head
Kathy Crispin, Section Head
Linda Graffam, Section Head
Jill Gravel, Section Head
Michele Johns, Staff
Carrie Kinne, Staff
Dodo Stevens, Section Head
Cris Tierney, Section Head

WINE PAIRINGS

Bob Crispin
Kevin Tierney

GRAPHIC DESIGN

Donnie O'Quinn
Leslie Wagner

DISTRIBUTION COMMITTEE

Linda Graffam
Ann Hibbard
Barbara Hoppin
Michele Johns
Carrie Kinne
Janine Manning
Jeff Nathanson
Patricia O'Carroll
Fran Philip
Nancy Pierce
Dodo Stevens

ART

Krista Alexander is a graphic designer and artist living in North Waterboro, Maine. She has illustrated and designed covers for several books including *Raindance, Cooking with Love, Glorious* and *Consider the Elephant*. A transplanted Southerner, much of Krista's artwork is inspired by the wonders of her adopted home.

We owe a special debt of gratitude to Maine Employers' Mutual Insurance Company for helping to underwrite the expenses of the printing this cookbook.

MEMIC
Partners for Workplace Safety™

Table of Contents

Appetizers

Appetizers

Reuben Dip

Serves 8 to 10

I package (8 ounce) cream cheese

2 tablespoons mayonnaise

2 tablespoons Russian dressing

2 tablespoons sour cream

Dash of garlic powder

8 ounces sauerkraut, drained

6 ounces corned beef, snipped into small pieces

4 ounces Cheddar cheese, grated

4 ounces Swiss cheese, chopped

Cocktail rye bread slices

Mix together in a 1½ quart casserole cream cheese, mayonnaise, dressing, sour cream and garlic powder. Add sauerkraut, corned beef and cheeses and mix well. Bake at 350°F for 20 to 25 minutes. Serve with rye bread slices.

Rich, but worth it!

Blue Cheese Dip

7 slices bacon, chopped

2 cloves garlic, minced

I package (8 ounce) cream cheese

¼ cup half-and-half

4 ounces or I cup blue cheese, crumbled

3 tablespoons salted almonds, chopped

Cook bacon in a skillet until almost crisp. Drain excess fat from skillet, add garlic, and cook until bacon is crisp. Preheat oven to 350°F. Beat cream cheese until smooth. Add half-and-half and mix until combined. Stir in bacon, garlic, and blue cheese. Transfer to 2-cup baking dish and cover in tinfoil. May be prepared one day ahead. Bring to room temperature before baking. Bake about 30 minutes, until heated through. Sprinkle with almonds.

Serve with sliced pears, apples, toasted pita chips, French bread.

Recipe Notes

Recipe Notes

Baked Artichoke Dip

I cup mayonnaise

I cup Parmesan cheese, grated

I can (14 ounce) artichoke hearts, drained

Juice of I lemon

I package zesty Italian dressing dry mix

3 tablespoons dry breadcrumbs

I teaspoon olive oil

Corn chips or crackers

Preheat oven to 400°F. Stir together mayonnaise and cheese. Finely chop artichoke hearts. Stir artichoke into the cheese mixture. Add lemon juice and Italian dressing mix. Place all mixed ingredients into a baking dish and spread evenly. Combine breadcrumbs and olive oil and sprinkle over top of dip. Bake until top is browned, about 20 minutes.

This recipe doubles and triples easily — a tasty version!

A variation:

I package (8 ounce) cream cheese, room temperature

I can (14 ounce) artichoke hearts, drained and chopped

I package (10 ounce) frozen chopped spinach, thawed and squeezed dry

$1/4$ cup mayonnaise

$1/2$ cup Parmesan cheese, grated

$1/4$ cup mozzarella cheese, grated

I clove garlic, minced

$1/2$ teaspoon basil, dried only

$1/4$ teaspoon garlic salt

Cream together cream cheese, mayonnaise, grated cheeses, garlic and garlic salt. Mix in artichokes and spinach. Mist pan with cooking oil spray. Cooking instructions same as above recipe but may take an extra 5 minutes in the oven.

You may want to add more mayonnaise, basil, garlic — depending on taste.

Hot and Spicy Spinach Dipping Sauce

Recipe Notes

2 (4 inch) hot green chiles, seeded and chopped

I (2 inch) jalapeño chile, seeded and minced

I small onion, chopped

2 tablespoons olive oil

2 tomatoes, peeled, seeded and chopped

I package (10 ounce) frozen chopped spinach, thawed and squeezed dry

I tablespoon red wine vinegar

I package (8 ounce) cream cheese, at room temperature

2 cups Monterey Jack cheese, grated

I cup half-and-half cream

Salt and pepper to taste

Cook chiles and onion in oil 4 minutes or until onions are soft. Add tomatoes, cook 2 minutes. Transfer to a bowl. Stir in spinach, vinegar, cream cheese, and other ingredients. Transfer to a buttered 10-inch ovenproof serving dish. Bake in preheated 400°F oven for 20 to 25 minutes or until hot and bubbly. Serve with tortilla chips.

Best when prepared one day ahead.

I suggest wearing gloves when working with chiles!

For a cold, but spicy version of this dip, blend in food processor 8 ounces of cream cheese, 1 cup of mayonnaise (you may use half sour cream), ¾ cup sliced scallions, ¼ cup chopped cilantro, 1 tablespoon chopped chipotle in adobo sauce, 1½ tablespoons freshly squeezed lime juice and ¾ teaspoon kosher salt until very smooth. Pulse in spinach (amount and preparation same as for Hot Spinach Dip) until just combined. Taste to adjust seasoning if necessary. Serve with tortilla chips.

Hot Spinach Dip

2 packages (10 ounce) chopped frozen spinach, thawed, squeezed dry

2 packages (8 ounce) cream cheese, cubed

2 packages (8 ounce) Monterey Jack cheese, shredded

2 cups salsa

²/₃ cup light cream

Mix all ingredients together. Place in 2 quart ovenproof dish. Bake at 350°F until bubbly. Serve with thinly sliced peasant bread, sliced apples or your favorite cracker.

Black Bean and Fresh Corn Dip

1 can (14½ ounce) black beans, drained

1½ cups fresh corn, cooked, cut from the cob or cooked frozen corn

1 medium red onion, chopped

2 tablespoons basil, chopped

1 red bell pepper, chopped

2 tablespoons lemon juice

1 tablespoon vegetable oil

Salt

Mix all together. Serve at room temperature with tortilla wedges or as a side dish for a summer beach barbeque.

This dip can also be turned into a salsa by adding diced mangoes.

Crab Dip

I package (8 ounce) cream cheese, softened

2 - 3 tablespoons milk

6$^{1}/_{2}$ ounces crabmeat

2 tablespoons onion, finely chopped

$^{1}/_{2}$ teaspoon horseradish

$^{1}/_{4}$ teaspoon salt

Pepper

Tabasco sauce (optional)

Mix well by hand and spoon into 2 quart ovenproof dish. Bake at 375°F for 15 minutes. Serve with toasted wedges of pita bread.

Layered Curried Cheese Spread

I package (8 ounce) cream cheese

4 ounces Cheddar cheese, shredded

I teaspoon curry powder

$^{1}/_{2}$ cup mango chutney

2 tablespoons coconut

$^{1}/_{4}$ cup pecans, chopped

2 tablespoons green onions, chopped

$^{1}/_{4}$ cup currants

Bring cream cheese to room temperature. Mix in Cheddar cheese (food processor works best). Blend in curry powder. Shape into ball then flatten into disk like Brie. Place in refrigerator for at least 1 hour. Just before serving, layer over cheese in order the chutney, coconut, pecans, green onion and currants.

A variation on the very popular crabmeat dip

I package (8 ounce) cream cheese, softened

16 ounces fresh crabmeat (you may use less and you may substitute canned)

$^{1}/_{2}$ cup mayonnaise

I teaspoon onion powder

I tablespoon powdered sugar

4 tablespoons sherry

Dash seasoned salt

Heat all the ingredients in a double boiler. Good to serve in a chafing dish. Serve with your favorite substantial cracker, pita bread wedges or toasted French bread slices.

You might consider substituting tapenade for the pesto. Here's a simple recipe, or you may purchase it pre-made in your favorite market.

Tapenade

2 teaspoons lemon juice

3 tablespoons capers

I clove garlic

I cup green or black olives (Kalamata olives, preferred)

5 anchovy fillets

Olive oil (optional)

Add ingredients to food processor and mix. Add olive oil if mixture is too dry. May also serve on toasted pita wedges.

Sun-Dried Tomato and Goat Cheese Crostini

Makes 60 to 80 slices

2 (12 inch) French baguettes

8 ounces pesto

I small container goat cheese (Brie can be substituted)

6-8 ounces sun-dried tomatoes in oil

Preheat oven to 350°F. Slice bread into ¼-inch slices. Arrange on cookie sheets. Spread a thin layer of pesto over each slice. Bake for 5 minutes. Remove from oven and cool slightly. Spread a thin layer of cheese over each slice. Top with a sun-dried tomato slice. Increase oven temperature to 400°F and bake for 10 minutes or until golden brown. Remove from oven and serve warm.

Bruschetta Bar

Grill slices (¼-inch thick) of baguettes until golden. Rub a garlic clove over toasted surface and drizzle with extra virgin olive oil. Arrange various toppings in a self serve "top your own bruschetta bar." Try to have a variety of color, taste, and texture; 5 to 6 toppings from the following options. Many of these can be purchased in the grocery store or in an Italian specialty store.

Roasted garlic cloves

Black olive tapenade

Yellow and/or red roasted peppers (thinly sliced)

Pesto

Grilled prosciutto

Goat cheese

Roasted tomatoes seeded and chopped, mixed with extra virgin olive oil and Italian herbs or chunky marinara sauce

Sun-dried tomatoes

Roasted eggplant

Arrange each topping in a small dish and allow guests to top their own (many can be mixed together e.g. goat cheese and prosciutto).

Recipe Notes

Chèvre & Pesto Torta

I cup basil pesto

$^{1}/_{2}$ cup sun-dried tomato purée

$^{1}/_{2}$ pound mascarpone or cream cheese

$^{1}/_{2}$ pound chèvre cheese

$^{1}/_{2}$ pound butter

Crostini or crackers for serving

Beat cheeses and butter together until smooth. Line bottom of 4 or 6-inch springform pan with ⅓ cheese mixture and top with pesto. Cover pesto with another layer of cheese mixture and cover cheese mixture with sun-dried tomato purée. Cover sun-dried tomato purée with the last ⅓ of cheese mixture and refrigerate 2 to 3 hours before serving. Unmold and serve with crostini or crackers.

This recipe may be frozen.

Mozzarella Cheese Puffs

I cup sifted flour

$^{1}/_{4}$ teaspoon salt

$^{1}/_{4}$ teaspoon paprika

$^{1}/_{2}$ cup butter or margarine

6 ounces mozzarella cheese, shredded

Sift dry ingredients together. Cream the butter and the cheese. Add the dry ingredients and mix well. Shape the mixture into 1-inch balls. Place them on a lightly greased baking sheet. Bake for 15 to 20 minutes at 350°F.

Different cheeses may be substituted — might use Cheddar and walnuts. Use your imagination!

Suggested wine: Proseco

Cheese Puffs

I loaf firm, unsliced bread

I package (3 ounces) cream cheese

¼ pound sharp Cheddar cheese

¼ pound butter

2 egg whites, beaten stiff

Trim crusts from bread and cut into 1-inch cubes. Melt cheese and butter in double boiler. Remove from heat and fold in the stiff egg whites. Dip cubes into mixture. Place on cookie sheet and refrigerate for 4 hours or overnight. Bake at 400°F for 12 to 15 minutes.

Blue Cheese Straws

6 ounces flour

3 ounces butter, cut into pieces

4 ounces Danish blue cheese

2 tablespoons cold water

Salt and pepper

Sift flour into a bowl and add a pinch of salt. Add butter. Rub together until mixture resembles breadcrumbs. Grate the cheese into the bowl and season with pepper. Add the water into the center of the mixture and blend with a fork. Place on a floured surface and knead gently. Refrigerate for 15 minutes before rolling with a floured rolling pin. Cut strips about 4 inches long by ¼-inch wide. Bake on a greased sheet at 400°F for 10 minutes. Allow time to cool on a rack before serving.

For a variation, use 1 cup finely grated Parmesan with ¼ teaspoon of cayenne pepper.

Suggested wine: Champagne

Champagne Cocktail

Serves 1

Drop a sugar cube into a champagne glass. Sprinkle with 1 to 2 dashes of bitters. Top with cold, dry champagne. Add a lemon twist for garnish.

Another Champagne Cocktail

Serves 10

Pour 2 bottles champagne or sparkling wine into pitcher. Add 1 cup raspberry flavored vodka. Add splash of grenadine. Chill. Pour into champagne glass and add a skewer with fresh raspberries for garnish. (Or drop a couple of fresh raspberries into the bottom of the glass, add the champagne.)

Stilton and Port Pies

I ounce unsalted butter

I package puff pastry, thawed

8 ounces cottage cheese

4 tablespoons milk

3 eggs, divided

2 tablespoons ruby port

Fresh ground pepper

6 ounces Stilton, rind removed and cheese cut into pieces

Salad greens as garnish

Preheat oven to 400°F. Lightly butter 12-hole muffin tin or 24-hole mini-tin. Lay out pastry and cut required circles with round cutter. To make filling, spoon cottage cheese into a bowl and beat until smooth with the milk. Add 1 egg and 1 egg yolk and port and beat well. Season with black pepper and then divide into muffin tin. Top each with nugget of Stilton and brush with 1 beaten egg. Bake for around 20 minutes or until set, and golden, and pastry is crisp.

Yummy! Worth the time to make.

Polenta Bites with Blue Cheese, Tomatoes and Pine Nuts

Makes 24

3 cups low-sodium chicken broth

I cup yellow cornmeal

I cup Parmesan cheese

2 ounces soft blue cheese, cubed, or use crumbled blue cheese to fill

3 tablespoons green onions, thinly sliced

2 tablespoons pine nuts, toasted

12 red grape tomatoes, quartered lengthwise

Chopped parsley

Use 2 non-stick 12 cup mini muffin tins (about 1¾ inches in diameter and ½-inch high sides). Bring broth to boil in medium saucepan over medium-high heat. Reduce heat to medium. Gradually whisk in cornmeal and cook until mixture is very thick, stirring constantly for about 2 minutes. Remove from heat. Stir in Parmesan cheese. Taste to see if you want more salt. Spoon 1½ tablespoons hot polenta into each muffin cup. Using back of spoon or thumb, press polenta firmly into cup. Using thumb, make indentation in center of each polenta cup for filling. Chill until cold and set, about 3 hours or overnight. Cover and keep chilled.

Preheat oven to 300°F. Line baking sheet with foil. Using tip of knife, lift polenta cups from pan and place on foil, indented side up. Place 1 blue cheese cube or a little crumbled blue cheese in indentation. Sprinkle green onion and pine nuts over cheese. Top each polenta cup with 2 tomato quarters. Bake until cheese is melted and polenta is warmed through. Sprinkle chopped parsley. Transfer to serving dish.

Garden Medley Cheese Bites

Recipe Notes

10 eggs

$^1/_2$ cup flour

$1^1/_2$ teaspoons onion powder

1 teaspoon baking powder

$^1/_2$ teaspoon garlic powder

$^1/_4$ cup butter, melted

3 cups cottage cheese, divided

1 cup cooked fresh spinach or 1 (10-ounce) package frozen chopped, thawed, squeezed dry

$^1/_2$ each red, yellow, and green pepper, chopped

$^1/_2$ green onion, chopped

12 ounces shredded Swiss or Monterey Jack cheese

Preheat oven to 350°F. In food processor combine eggs, flour, baking powder, onion powder, garlic powder, butter, and half the cottage cheese. Pour blended mixture into large bowl and add remaining cottage cheese, as well as remaining ingredients and mix.

Pour into a greased 9x11-inch pan and bake for 45 minutes until set. Cool before cutting.

Tomato Tarts

1 sheet frozen puff pastry, thawed

¼ cup pesto (or to taste)

1 cup mozzarella cheese, grated

½ cup Parmesan cheese, grated

1½ pounds tomatoes, sliced thin

1 small red onion, sliced thin and halved

2 teaspoons fresh rosemary leaves, chopped

2 teaspoons fresh thyme leaves, chopped

Preheat oven to 425°F. On a lightly floured surface, with a rolling pin, roll out pastry into a rectangle of approximately 16x14 inches. Halve pastry lengthwise, forming two (16x7-inch) rectangles. Brush edges with water and fold edges in to create a ½-inch wide border around each rectangle. Seal border by pressing down with a fork. Transfer rectangles to a large baking sheet. Divide pesto between rectangles and spread into thin layer. Sprinkle each tart evenly with a ½ cup mozzarella cheese and 2 tablespoons Parmesan cheese. Arrange tomato slices in one layer on cheese. Season the tomatoes with salt and pepper. Scatter onion slices and herbs over tomatoes and sprinkle with remaining ¼ cup Parmesan cheese.

Bake tarts in oven for approximately 12 to 15 minutes, or until crust is golden brown. Slice into individual servings. May be served warm or at room temperature.

Recipe Notes

Spinach Canapés

4 boxes of frozen chopped spinach

1 pound shredded Monterey Jack cheese

1 cup milk

1 stick butter

1 cup shredded Parmesan cheese

3 eggs

$^{1}/_{4}$ cup flour

$^{1}/_{2}$ teaspoon salt

Thaw and squeeze moisture out of spinach, and dry with a paper towel. Beat eggs, salt and onion; add flour and milk; then add jack cheese and spinach. Mix well. Melt butter in 9x12-inch pan. Pour spinach mixture in pan and press down. Sprinkle with Parmesan. Bake at 325°F for 45 minutes. Cool and cut in cubes. Serve immediately or you may freeze in bags after separated. Remove from freezer, re-bake on cookie sheet at 350°F for 10 to 15 minutes.

Cut in larger wedges, this would make a nice side dish with a simple grilled meat entrée.

Asparagus Wraps

Makes 40 to 60

20 slices white sandwich bread

3/4 pound butter

4 ounces blue cheese, at room temperature

1 package (**8** ounce) cream cheese, at room temperature

1 egg, beaten

20 fresh asparagus spears

Trim crusts from bread and flatten slightly with a rolling pin. In a bowl, stir together the blue and cream cheeses with egg until well blended and creamy. Spread a thin layer of the cheese mixture over each slice of bread. Roll one asparagus spear inside and fasten with a toothpick, if needed. Melt butter in a small saucepan. Roll each asparagus wrap in butter to coat. Place on a baking sheet small enough to fit in the freezer and freeze for 1 hour or until butter hardens and wraps are somewhat firm. Remove pan from freezer, discard toothpicks and cut each wrap in half or thirds. Store in a re-sealable plastic bag in the freezer until ready to use. To serve, preheat oven to 400°F. Arrange frozen asparagus wraps on an ungreased baking sheet. Bake in the preheated oven for 15 to 20 minutes, depending on oven, or until lightly browned. Check occasionally and turn if necessary to brown evenly and prevent burning.

This recipe doubles and triples easily.

Huge favorite at Portland Yacht Club events — they always disappear!

Recipe Notes

Mushrooms Stuffed with Tofu and Walnuts

Makes 12 mushrooms

1 medium onion, minced

3 cloves garlic, minced

$1/4$ cup olive oil, divided

14 ounces firm tofu

$1/2$ teaspoon rosemary, crumbled

2 small tomatoes, chopped

$1/3$ cup walnuts, ground

2 teaspoons miso

$1/2$ teaspoon balsamic vinegar

2 tablespoons tomato paste

12 large cremini or other type of mushroom, stems removed

$1/4$ cup scallions, chopped

To prepare tofu: buy firm and freeze overnight. Defrost. The freezing step changes the texture to a meaty texture. This allows for the flavors in the recipe to be absorbed. Once defrosted, pat dry with paper towel to remove excess water.

Preheat oven to 350°F. In large skillet, add 2 tablespoons oil and sauté onions and garlic. Crumble tofu over onions and sauté an additional 5 minutes. Add the rosemary and tomatoes and cook over low heat for 10 minutes or until mixture is fairly dry. Add the walnuts, miso, vinegar, tomato paste and salt and pepper. Drizzle with 2 tablespoons oil. Place mushrooms in baking dish and fill each with 1 tablespoon stuffing. Press to firmly pack.

Bake for 20 minutes. Before serving, sprinkle with chopped scallions. Serve warm.

Stuffed Mushrooms with Tarragon

Serves 6 to 12

I pound of fresh mushrooms	$1/4$ cup shredded Swiss cheese
3 tablespoons shallots or onions	$1/4$ cup Parmesan cheese
4 tablespoons butter	4 tablespoons parsley
$1/2$ cup sherry	$1/2$ teaspoons tarragon
3 tablespoons breadcrumbs	2 3 tablespoons cream or milk

Brush and clean mushrooms and remove stems. Mince mushroom stems and shallots. Sauté shallots in 2 tablespoons of butter for 2 to 3 minutes. Add sherry and minced stems and simmer until reduced.

Mix breadcrumbs, Swiss and Parmesan cheeses, parsley, tarragon and cream. Remove mushroom stems from heat and add to breadcrumb mixture.

Brush mushroom caps with melted butter and fill caps. Bake at 375°F for 12 to 15 minutes.

If you're a fan of tarragon like I am I always add extra. You may also top with shredded Swiss cheese before baking.

These are simple and different than other stuffed mushroom recipes.

Try these variations:

24 medium mushrooms, stems removed and finely chopped

$1/4$ cup dry breadcrumbs

$1/2$ cup lump crabmeat or finely chopped prosciutto or crumbled cooked bacon

$1/2$ cup freshly grated Parmesan cheese, Asiago or crumbled feta, $1/4$ cup reserved

I egg, lightly beaten

2 tablespoons olive oil or melted butter

Salt and freshly ground pepper

Preheat oven to 375°F. Arrange mushroom caps in a single layer in a lightly greased shallow pan. In a bowl combine $1/2$ cup chopped stems, breadcrumbs, meat, cheese and egg. Divide among mushroom caps, mounding slightly. Drizzle with oil or butter, top with reserved cheese and bake 12 to 15 minutes or until heated through.

Recipe Notes

Stuffed Dates Wrapped in Bacon

Makes 2 dozen

2 containers medjool dates

¹/₃ cup ricotta cheese

1 pound bacon

Pit the dates by making a small slice at either end and pushing the pit through with a wooden skewer or other small kitchen tool.

If you don't have a pastry bag, open a plastic sandwich bag in a measuring cup and fill bag with the ricotta cheese. Snip off small corner and squeeze ricotta into each date until the cheese comes out of the other end.

Cut bacon strips in half. Wrap ½ strip of bacon around each date and secure with toothpick. Place on baking sheet and roast in 450°F oven for 15 to 20 minutes.

Can be made a few hours ahead and kept in the refrigerator.

Sweet and savory. This is an easy appetizer derived from Spanish tapas.

Hot Zucchini Squares

3 cups zucchini, unpeeled, thinly sliced

I cup biscuit baking mix

$1/2$ cup onion, finely chopped

$1/3$ cup Parmesan cheese, grated

2 tablespoons parsley, snipped

$1/2$ teaspoon salt

$1/2$ teaspoon dried oregano

Dash of pepper

I clove garlic, finely chopped

$1/2$ cup vegetable oil

4 eggs, slightly beaten

Preheat oven to 350°F. Grease 9x13-inch pan. Mix all ingredients well. Pour into pan and spread evenly. Bake until golden brown, about 25 minutes. Cut into 4 dozen squares.

Everyone loves this recipe and it is a delicious way to use the sometimes over abundant zucchini harvest of the summer season.

Chile Cheese Squares

I can (4 ounces) diced chiles, drained

I cup biscuit baking mix

I cup light cream

4 eggs

$1/4$ teaspoon salt

10 ounces mozzarella cheese, shredded

Mix all ingredients. Bake in 9x12-inch pan at 375°F for 45 minutes. Let cool and then slice into cubes. If freezing, separate cubes on sheet. When frozen, place in bags. Place frozen squares on cookie sheet and bake for 10 minutes.

Do not double — will not cook well.

Recipe Notes

Recipe Notes

Spicy Sausage Meatballs

2 pounds bulk pork sausage

1 pound lean ground beef

4 eggs, beaten

1½ cups soft breadcrumbs

3 cups ketchup

½ cup white vinegar

½ cup soy sauce

Mix meats, eggs and breadcrumbs. Form bite-sized balls. Sauté in frying pan until brown, drain. Combine the remaining ingredients and pour over the sausage balls, simmer for 30 minutes.

May use 3 pounds of sausage and omit hamburger. Freezes well, so make ahead and keep on hand.

Big hit at our house and a must have on Christmas Eve.

Sausage Cheese Bites

1 pound hot or sweet Italian sausage, casing removed

1 pound sharp Cheddar cheese, grated

3 cups biscuit baking mix

¾ cup water

Brown, crumble and drain sausage. Mix with remaining ingredients and form 1-inch balls. Bake for 15 to 20 minutes at 350°F on an ungreased baking sheet. Serve warm. If freezing to serve later, place on clean baking sheet. When frozen, place in freezer bag. If serving from frozen, bake at 350°F for 10 minutes.

This is an excellent appetizer to keep in the freezer for unexpected guests. Works well on the deck or in front of the fire!

Suggested wine: Gewürztraminer

Prosciutto Pinwheels

I package puff pastry sheets

³/₄ cup Dijon mustard

³/₄ pound prosciutto ham, thinly sliced

I cup Monterey Jack cheese, shredded

I cup sharp Cheddar cheese, shredded

Thaw two sheets of pastry (1 package). Spread Dijon mustard on each pastry sheet. Spread ham evenly on the two sheets. Sprinkle cheeses on each sheet. Roll the sheet up on the long side and pinch closed. Refrigerate or freeze. When ready to cook, slice chilled roll into ½-inch slices. Place face down on a greased cookie sheet and cook for 10 to 15 minutes at 375°F.

This freezes very well. Best if baked on parchment paper or new non-stick aluminum foil (do not use regular foil as they may stick). Easiest way to slice is when these are partially frozen.

May substitute shredded provolone for the cheeses.

Prosciutto, Arugula and Gorgonzola Wraps

Makes 16 wraps

3-4 ounces Gorgonzola dolce (if unavailable you may use any Gorgonzola or a container of crumbled Gorgonzola)

I bunch or package of baby arugula

16 slices prosciutto (sliced thin and fresh from the market)

$^1/_2$ cup currants (optional)

Fresh figs, when in season

If you are using a container of crumbled Gorgonzola, mix with 2 tablespoons cream cheese for a softer consistency. Wash and dry arugula. Pick out the leaves of similar size and good color.

Carefully peel 1 slice of prosciutto and lay horizontally on work surface. Place 2 or 3 small arugula leaves together on one end of the slice with the wide leaves on top and slightly above the ham. Place 1½ teaspoons Gorgonzola on bottom ends of arugula, sprinkle a few currants and carefully roll the prosciutto until a little wrap is formed. Make sure the arugula remains visible and forms a little green bouquet. If your slice of prosciutto is too long, you might cut it in half and make 2 wraps.

Serve on a beautiful platter with the wraps surrounding a mound of quartered fresh figs.

Perfection on a platter!

Garlic Chicken Mini Pizzas

Makes 4 pizzas

¹/₄ cup plus 2 tablespoons olive oil, divided

2 large onions, thinly sliced

3 tablespoons brown sugar

1¹/₂ tablespoons apple cider vinegar

1¹/₂ teaspoons garlic, minced plus 1 tablespoon garlic, minced

1 pound skinless boneless chicken thigh, cut into very small pieces

2 tablespoons Thai chili garlic sauce

6 tablespoons fresh cilantro, chopped, divided

2 tubes (10 ounce) pizza dough

1 cup mozzarella cheese, shredded

¹/₂ cup Swiss cheese, shredded

¹/₂ cup Provolone cheese, shredded

3 plum tomatoes, seeded and chopped

You might substitute cooked Italian sausage or prosciutto for the chicken, chili, garlic and cilantro. Add some mushrooms to the onion…experiment!

Heat ¼ cup oil in skillet over high heat. Add onions and sauté for 5 minutes. Reduce heat to medium low and sauté until onions are dark brown, about 25 minutes. Add sugar, vinegar and 1½ teaspoons garlic. Stir until liquid evaporates and onions are glazed, about 2 minutes longer. Season with salt and pepper. Cool.

Heat 2 tablespoons oil in heavy, large skillet over medium-high heat. Add chicken and sauté for about 2 minutes. Add 1 tablespoon garlic and sauté for an additional 2 minutes. Add Thai chili sauce and sauté 1 minute. Remove chicken and stir in half the chopped cilantro.

Preheat oven to 450°F. Stretch dough from 1 tube into 12x8 rectangle. Cut crosswise in half to form 2 (6x8 inch) rectangles. Transfer to lightly floured (or cornmeal) baking sheet. Repeat with second tube of dough. Bake until tops are light brown, about 8 minutes.

Mix cheeses together. Sprinkle cheese mixture, tomatoes, onions, chicken and remaining cilantro over pizzas, dividing evenly. Bake pizzas until cheese melts, about 5 minutes longer.

Recipe Notes

Portobello Mushrooms with Shrimp

4 to 8 servings

1/4 cup olive oil

1/2 cup chopped onions

1/4 cup chopped basil

4 large garlic cloves, chopped

1/2 teaspoon fresh rosemary, chopped

8 ounces raw shrimp, peeled and de-veined and coarsely chopped

2/3 cup panko breadcrumbs

1/2 cup grated Parmesan cheese

1/4 cup mayonnaise

8 (2 to 2 1/2 inch) Portobello mushrooms (remove gills)

Preheat oven to 350°F. Heat oil in large skillet over medium high heat. Add onion, basil, garlic and rosemary. Sauté until onions soften, about 5 minutes, add shrimp and sauté until shrimp are pink. Transfer to bowl and mix in breadcrumbs, cheese and mayonnaise. Season with salt and pepper.

Arrange mushrooms on lightly oiled baking sheet. Mound filling into mushrooms, pressing to compact slightly. Bake mushrooms until tender, about 35 minutes. Serve hot.

You may substitute crabmeat for the shrimp.

With a green salad, this will make a light lunch.

Shrimp, Scallop and Spinach Turnovers

3 tablespoons butter

8 ounces mushrooms, sliced

⅓ cup shallots, chopped

I cup whipping cream

½ cup dry white wine

½ cup chicken broth

1½ tablespoons Dijon mustard

I teaspoon white wine vinegar

I package (IO ounce) frozen, chopped spinach, thawed, squeezed dry

I package frozen puff pastry (2 sheets), thawed

16 raw, large shrimp, peeled, deveined; cut into bite size pieces

8 sea scallops, cut into bite size pieces

Preheat oven to 500°F. Melt butter in skillet over medium-high heat. Add mushrooms and shallots, sauté for about 5 minutes. Add cream, wine and chicken broth. Boil until mixture is reduced to 1 cup. Mix in mustard and vinegar. Add spinach. Season with salt and pepper and cool.

Roll out 1 pastry sheet to create a 12-inch square. Cut into 4 even squares. Place ⅛ of spinach mixture near center of square. Top spinach mixture with ⅛ of the cut shrimp and scallops. Brush pastry edges with water to help seal edges. Fold unfilled half of pastry over filling, forming triangle. Press edges closed with fork. Place pastry on large baking dish. Repeat with remaining pastry and filling.

Bake the pastries for 5 minutes. Reduce heat to 375°F and continue to bake for 15 more minutes or until golden brown.

Make the filling ahead of time (earlier in day and refrigerate); can substitute puff pastry for phyllo dough; can also use mini puff pastry shells.

Cajun Shrimp

2 pounds raw shrimp (16 to 20 count size preferred), may be fresh or frozen

MARINADE

$^1/_2$ cup extra virgin olive oil

Juice of 1 lemon

2 tablespoons soy sauce

$^1/_4$ cup brown sugar

6 to 8 cloves garlic

1 tablespoon Cajun seasoning or more to taste

Coat thawed shrimp and marinate 2 hours to overnight. You may either grill, broil or bake (350°F for about 10 minutes or until pink).

Lobster Bundles

Makes 24

1 scallion

8 ounces lobster meat, cooked

$^1/_4$ cup feta cheese, crumbled

1 tablespoon Dijon mustard

4 ounces cream cheese, softened

1 tablespoon fresh tarragon

1 tablespoon white wine

24 wonton wrappers (3x3)

Salt and pepper to taste

Vegetable cooking spray

Preheat oven to 375°F. Trim and slice scallion, using green part only. In a medium bowl, toss lobster with scallion and feta. Mix with mustard, cream cheese, salt, pepper, tarragon and wine. Spray mini muffin tins with vegetable spray. Place wonton wrapper in each cup and press gently. Place a heaping teaspoon of lobster mixture in the middle of each wonton. Fold in sides and twist to enclose. Spray bundle with vegetable spray lightly. Bake for 12 to 15 minutes or until lightly brown. Serve immediately.

Can prepare without muffin tin and place bundles on cookie sheet.

Mustard Prawns

4 tablespoons Dijon mustard

1/2 cup white wine vinegar

2 teaspoons salt

Dash black pepper

4 tablespoons finely chopped shallots

4 tablespoons finely chopped parsley

2 teaspoons ground red pepper flakes

1 1/2 teaspoons finely chopped tarragon

1/2 cup olive oil

2 pounds large prawns (26 - 30 count)

If prawns are purchased raw, place in boiling, salted water. When water returns to a boil, prawns should be done. Do not overcook. Drain and peel.

Combine mustard, vinegar, salt, pepper, shallots, parsley, red pepper flakes and tarragon and slowly whisk in ½ cup olive oil. Sauce should be thick and creamy. Combine with prawns and refrigerate overnight. Serve with skewers as hors d'oeuvres or arrange on a plate with lettuce and garnish with chopped chives for a first course. Sauce may be dribbled over lettuce as dressing.

Timesaving hint: you may purchase frozen or unfrozen cooked shrimp, just remove the tails and place in marinade.

Halibut Kabobs

Makes 16 skewers

Recipe Notes

2 medium zucchinis

2 pounds halibut, cut into 1½-inch cubes

1 container grape tomatoes

1 lemon

¼+ cup olive oil, divided

2 teaspoons dried oregano

16 wooden skewers (soaked in water at least ½ hour)

Slice zucchini lengthwise in half and then in ½-inch moons. Sauté in 2 tablespoons olive oil until softened but not brown, 5 to 7 minutes.

Make marinade with remainder of olive oil, zest from the lemon and lemon juice. Add salt and pepper and oregano. Add grape tomatoes, cooked zucchini and halibut to marinade, toss and let marinate 1 hour in the refrigerator.

To assemble, thread ingredients on well-soaked skewers and grill either indoors on a grill pan or outside on the barbeque grill for 7 to 9 minutes.

Suggested wine: Sauvignon Blanc

Thai Mussels

Serves 6 as an appetizer or 2 as a meal

¼ cup butter

4 tomatoes, seeded and chopped

2 tablespoons garlic, minced

2 tablespoons fresh ginger, peeled and chopped

2 cans (14 ounces) unsweetened coconut milk

2 tablespoons Thai red curry paste

1 bunch fresh cilantro, chopped

1 teaspoon salt

3 pounds mussels, scrubbed clean

Melt butter in large heavy pot over medium-high heat. Add tomatoes, garlic and ginger; sauté until garlic is tender, about 2 minutes. Add in coconut milk, curry paste, salt and cilantro, reserving some cilantro for garnish. Simmer 5 minutes to blend flavors. Add mussels; cover and cook until mussels open, about 5 minutes. Discard any mussels that do not open. Transfer mixture to serving bowl and add garnish.

Serve with plenty of crusty fresh bread to soak up the delicious sauce.

How to debeard mussels:

Clean mussels by scrubbing them under cold water with a brush. Scrape off any barnacles with a knife. If the beard is still attached, remove by pulling it from the tip to hinge or by pulling and cutting it off with a knife. Mussels die shortly after the beards are removed. Cook shortly after debearding them.

Tuna and Avocado Tartare on Wonton Crisps

Serves 8

There are two ways to serve this. You can spoon tartare into a bowl, sprinkle with chives (and toasted sesame seeds) and surround with crisps for dipping or spooning. Or, for a more elegant presentation, you can make individual canapés and sprinkle each with chives and sesame seeds.

CRISPS

12 wonton wrappers, cut in half diagonally

Olive oil

Toasted sesame seeds (optional)

Preheat oven to 350°F. Arrange wonton triangles on baking sheet, brush each with oil (sprinkle with sesame seeds). Bake until slightly golden brown about 6 to 8 minutes. Watch carefully, they burn quickly. Cool on sheet. Can be made a few hours ahead.

TARTARE

2 tablespoons soy sauce

1 tablespoon rice vinegar

1 - 2 teaspoons wasabi paste

1 tablespoon sesame oil

1 tablespoon fresh lime juice

8 ounces sushi-grade Ahi tuna, cut into $^1/_3$-inch cubes

1 Haas avocado, halved, peeled and cut into $^1/_3$-inch cubes

$^2/_3$ cup seedless cucumber, chopped

1 green onion, thinly sliced

Chopped fresh chives

Whisk first 5 ingredients in a bowl. Add tuna, avocado, cucumber and green onion; stir gently to coat.

For a slightly different flavor, substitute finely chopped jalapeño pepper instead of green onion and add ½ chopped cilantro.

Soups & Stews

Soups & Stews

Gazpacho

Serves 6 to 8

8 large, ripe tomatoes

¼ cup good olive oil

¼ cup red wine vinegar

2 cloves of garlic, minced

I red onion, chopped finely

2 cucumbers, peeled, seeded and chopped

I green bell pepper, minced

I dash hot sauce

¼ teaspoon salt

½ lemon, juiced

Recipe Notes

Blanch the tomatoes in a pot of boiling water for 20 seconds or until skins begin to pucker. Remove immediately and plunge them into ice water. Peel the tomatoes when cooled. Place half the tomatoes in a blender or food processor. Pulse for several seconds until puréed. In a large bowl add the puréed tomatoes, the remaining tomatoes, diced and cored, and all the remaining ingredients. Mix together thoroughly. Cover and refrigerate overnight. Serve chilled.

Recipe Notes

Chilled Curried Cucumber Soup

Serves 6 as first course

1 cup loosely packed cilantro leaves (reserve a few leaves for garnish)

1 onion, quartered

2 large cucumbers, peeled, quartered lengthwise, seeded and cut into chunks

$1/2$ cup sour cream

$1^1/2$ cups plain, low-fat yogurt, divided

1 teaspoon curry

$1/4$ teaspoon salt

$1/4$ teaspoon white pepper

3 - 5 drops hot red sauce

$1^1/4$ cups unsalted vegetable or chicken stock

Chop cilantro in a food processor. Add the onion and cucumber chunks and process them until they are finely chopped but not puréed. (Alternately, chop the cilantro by hand and grate or finely chop the onion and cucumbers.) In a bowl, whisk the sour cream with 1 cup of the yogurt, curry powder, salt, white pepper and red-sauce. Whisk in the cucumber mixture and the stock. Refrigerate the soup for at least one hour. Serve the soup in chilled bowls. Garnish each portion with a dollop of the remaining yogurt and the reserved cilantro leaves.

Maine Blueberry Soup

Serves 6

I pint fresh Maine blueberries	I lemon, rind and juice
2 cups of water	$^1/_2$ cup fruity white wine
$^1/_2$ cup sugar	2 cups sour cream
I (3 inch) stick of cinnamon	

Rinse and drain blueberries, then put them in a large pot. Add water, sugar, cinnamon, lemon rind and lemon juice. Bring the soup to a boil, then reduce heat and simmer uncovered for 15 minutes. Remove the cinnamon stick. Reserve ⅓ cup of the blueberries. Purée remaining berries and rind, strain through a sieve. Refrigerate the soup until it is very cold. Before serving, stir in the wine and then beat in the sour cream. Add and gently stir in the reserved blueberries.

Recipe Notes

Recipe Notes

Roasted Leek and Potato Soup

Serves 4

3 tablespoons olive oil

4 leeks, washed, white parts only, chopped into 1 inch pieces

1¹/₂ cups Yukon gold potatoes, thinly sliced

2 tablespoons unsalted butter

1 onion, chopped

2¹/₂ cups vegetable stock

¹/₂ teaspoon salt

¹/₂ teaspoon pepper

1 cup light cream

¹/₄ cup chopped chives for garnish

Preheat oven to 450°F. Toss the chopped leeks in the olive oil and roast for 20 minutes. While the leeks are roasting, sauté the onions in the unsalted butter for about ten minutes, do not let them brown. Add potatoes, vegetable stock, salt and pepper and bring to a boil, then turn heat down to simmer. Cook gently for 20 minutes. Add the roasted leeks and simmer another 5 minutes until the vegetables are tender. Cool slightly, then whirl in a blender or food processor until smooth, or rub through a sieve. If soup is to be served hot, return to saucepan, add the cream and heat through, do not allow to boil. If serving cold, stir in cream and chill for ar least 2 hours. Garnish with chopped chives when ready to serve.

Roasted Squash, Onion and Garlic Soup

Serves 4 to 6

I unpeeled garlic head

2 pounds butternut squash or other orange flesh winter squash, unpeeled and cut into 8 pieces, seeds removed

I large onion, peeled and cut vertically in half

2 tablespoons olive oil

8 fresh thyme sprigs or 2 teaspoons dried, crumbled

1/2 cup whipping cream

1³/₄ cups chicken or vegetable stock

Minced parsley

Preheat oven to 350°F. Cut ⅓ inch off top of garlic head, exposing cloves. Arrange garlic, squash and onion, cut side up, in a large baking dish. Drizzle vegetables with oil. Scatter thyme over top. Cover dish tightly with foil and bake until squash is tender when pierced with a knife, about 1½ hours. Uncover vegetables and cool 15 minutes.

Scrape squash from skin into a food processor work bowl. Peel outer layers and trim root end from onion halves. Add onion to food processor. Separate 9 garlic cloves from head. Peel and add to processor. Add any juices from bottom of baking dish. Add cream and purée until almost smooth, scraping down sides of bowl occasionally. Taste, adding more garlic if stronger flavor is desired.

Transfer purée to a heavy, large saucepan. Whisk in 1¼ cups stock. Stir over medium heat until heated through, adding more broth if thinner consistency is desired. Season with salt and pepper. Can be made one day ahead. Cover and chill. Rewarm before serving.

Ladle into warm bowls and garnish with parsley and serve.

Recipe Notes

Recipe Notes

Butternut Squash Bisque

Serves 4 to 6

2 tablespoons butter

I small onion, minced

I - 2 pound butternut squash, peeled, seeded and cut into I inch pieces

I Golden Delicious apple, chopped

I quart low sodium chicken stock or vegetable stock

I bay leaf

I sprig thyme

I tablespoon honey

I cup heavy cream

$^1/_4$ cup Cheddar, Asiago or fontina cheese, grated (optional)

Melt the butter in a large pot over medium heat. Add onions and sauté until translucent. Add the squash and the apple and sauté for a few more minutes. Increase heat to high. Cover the apple and squash mixture with the stock. Add the bay leaf, thyme, and honey. Bring to a boil, reduce to simmer until squash is very soft, about 15 minutes. Remove bay leaf and thyme. Working in batches, purée the soup in a food processor or blender or run it though a sieve. Return soup to a pot. Add salt and pepper to taste. Add cream and if desired, the cheese. Stir over low heat until the cheese is melted and the soup is warm.

Red Pepper Bisque

Serves 4 to 6

2 tablespoons olive oil

1 onion, chopped

1 leek, white part only, chopped

2 medium sweet potatoes

1 cup water

1 large jar roasted red peppers, drained

4 cups chicken or vegetable broth

Salt and pepper to taste

1 cup cooked brown rice

Heat olive oil in a large pan over medium heat. Add onions and leeks and sauté until the onion is translucent. Add sweet potatoes, peppers, broth and water. Simmer until the sweet potatoes are tender. Using an immersion blender or food processor, blend until smooth. Add salt and pepper to taste. Ladle into serving bowls and top with a generous spoonful of brown rice.

Tarascan Soup

Serves 8

1 tablespoon olive oil

1 cup onion, chopped

5 large garlic cloves, minced

1 can (28 ounce) diced tomatoes, drained

2 cans (15 ounce) pinto beans, drained

2 teaspoons chili powder

$3/4$ teaspoon cumin

$1/2$ teaspoon hot sauce

$1/4$ teaspoon salt

2 cups chicken broth

Heat oil in a large pan over medium high heat. Add onions and sauté until onions are translucent. Add the garlic and sauté 2 minutes more. Stir in tomatoes and cook 5 minutes. Place beans in a blender or food processor and process until smooth. Add beans, chili powder, hot sauce, salt and broth to pan. Bring to a boil. Reduce heat to medium low and cook 18 minutes.

Serve with warm tortilla chips.

Recipe Notes

Sister Soup

Serves 6 to 8

3 quarts chicken broth

4 medium potatoes, peeled and diced

4 carrots, sliced

$1/2$ pound fresh string beans, halved

I large onion, diced

$1/2$ pound zucchini, cubed

I can (14 ounce) kidney beans, drained and rinsed

2 cups cooked chicken, bite-sized

Salt and pepper to taste

Bring broth, potatoes, carrots, green beans, onions, salt and pepper to a boil in a large soup pot. Reduce heat and simmer for 10 minutes. Add zucchini, kidney beans and chicken to pot. Simmer another 10 minutes or until vegetables are just tender.

PESTO

I can (6 ounce) tomato paste

4 cloves garlic, minced

$1/2$ cup fresh basil, minced

$1/2$ cup fresh parsley, minced

$1/4$ cup Parmesan cheese

$1/4$ cup olive oil

Combine ingredients for pesto in a small bowl or food processor. Just before serving, stir pesto into soup.

This soup is simple and flavorful. It's great for several days.

Jane Staley's Own Homespun Vegetable Barley Soup

Serves 8 to 10

I tablespoon olive oil

I pound lean ground beef

I¹/₂ cups diced potatoes

I¹/₂ cups diced celery

I¹/₂ cups diced carrots

I¹/₂ cups shredded cabbage

I¹/₂ cups diced green bell pepper

I¹/₂ cups minced onions

I¹/₂ cups chopped mushrooms

¹/₂ cup chopped parsley

2 bay leaves

I clove of garlic, minced

Sweet corn cut from 3 or 4 cobs

4 tomatoes, diced

2 cans of tomato paste

I can (16 ounce) beans
(either black, pinto or kidney)

I package frozen lima beans

I package frozen julienne green beans

4 cups chicken broth or tomato juice

I tablespoon arrowroot

I¹/₂ cups cooked barley

Heat the oil in a large pot over medium high heat. Add the hamburger and cook until it is not pink. Add all the remaining ingredients and bring to a boil. Reduce heat, cover, and simmer for 2 hours. Skim any fat from the surface of the soup. Dissolve the arrowroot in ½ cup of the thoroughly cooled soup stock and stir into soup. Add cooked barley.

Recipe Notes

Tuscan Soup

Serves 6 to 8

½ cup olive oil

I large onion, chopped

2 cloves of garlic, minced

2 stalks of celery, chopped

3 carrots, peeled and sliced

I cup cabbage, chopped

2 large potatoes, peeled and diced

8 cups vegetable or chicken broth

2 cups Tuscan kale or Swiss chard

I cup dried cannelloni beans

I cup tomatoes, chopped

2 bay leaves

2 tablespoons each of fresh parsley and basil

Salt and pepper to taste

Small sized pasta (optional)

Heat oil in a large pan over medium high heat and sauté onions until translucent, about 6 minutes. Add garlic and sauté another 2 minutes. Add carrots, cabbage, potatoes, Tuscan kale, beans, tomatoes and herbs and the broth. Bring to a boil and then reduce heat to simmer. Cook slowly for several hours until the beans are cooked. Season with salt and pepper. If desired, small sized pasta can be added at the end of cooking time.

Serve with crusty bread.

Broccoli with Blue Cheese Soup

Serves 4

I medium onion, finely chopped

I tablespoon oil

I large potato, peeled and cubed

I¹/₂ pints vegetable stock

I pound broccoli florets

3¹/₂ ounces blue cheese, cubed

Plain yogurt or heavy cream for garnish (optional)

In a large saucepan, heat oil. Add the onion and sauté until onion is soft but not browned. Add potato and stock to the pot and gently bring to a boil. Simmer for 15 minutes or until the potatoes are cooked. Add the broccoli florets and simmer another 10 minutes or until broccoli is cooked. Purée the soup in a food processor or immersion blender until it is smooth. Add the cubed blue cheese and allow to melt. Stir to mix in the cheese. Add salt and pepper to taste. If soup is too thick, add a little milk and gently reheat.

Serve with a swirl of plain yogurt or heavy cream.

Recipe Notes

Recipe Notes

Winter Minestrone

Serves 6

1 chopped onion	3 cups water
³/₄ pound lean ground beef	¹/₂ - 1 cup ripe olives, sliced
1 small eggplant, diced	¹/₂ cup small shell pasta
2 teaspoons garlic, minced	1 tablespoon minced parsley
2 carrots, sliced	1 teaspoon minced basil
15 ounces tomato purée	Salt and pepper to taste
2 cans (14 ounce) beef broth	Grated Parmesan cheese

Sauté onions and beef in a large heavy pot over medium heat until meat is cooked. Add eggplant, garlic, carrots, tomato purée, beef broth and water. Bring to a boil and simmer covered for 15 minutes or until the vegetables are cooked. Add olives, pasta, parsley and basil and season with salt and pepper to taste. Simmer 10 minutes more until the pasta is tender. Ladle the soup into bowls and garnish with grated Parmesan cheese.

Hamburger Soup

Serves 6

2 tablespoons olive oil

1½ pounds ground beef

1 medium onion, chopped

1 can (28 ounce) tomatoes

16 ounces beef broth

1 cup water

4 celery ribs, diced

4 large carrots, sliced

1 teaspoon thyme

1 teaspoon salt

½ cup quick cooking barley

¼ cup chopped parsley

In a large, heavy saucepan, heat the oil over medium heat. Add the onion and hamburger and cook until there is no longer pink in the beef. Drain off any excess fat. Stir in tomatoes, broth, water and add the celery and carrots. Stir in thyme and salt. Bring to a boil, then reduce heat and simmer covered for 45 minutes. Stir in barley and cook 5 more minutes.

Serve with crusty bread.

Recipe Notes

Hearty Sausage and Chicken Soup

(a.k.a. - An Afternoon with Football Stew!)

Serves 8

This is a wonderfully easy soup to prepare, and like all soups, it can be easily adjusted to the individual's liking — or refrigerator contents for that matter! By using hot sausage, the soup takes on an entirely different taste.

6 - 8 sweet or hot sausage links, removed from casing

4 - 5 chicken thighs

1 or 2 potatoes, peeled and cubed

1 large sweet onion, diced

1 cup fresh mushrooms, sliced

1 can (10 ounce) diced tomatoes

6 cups vegetable or chicken stock

1 can black beans, drained and rinsed

1 large sprig rosemary or about 1 tablespoon dried

1 tablespoon dried paprika

2 - 3 bay leaves

Salt and pepper

In large stockpot, brown the onions and mushrooms with olive oil, rosemary and paprika. Add the stock, tomatoes, diced potatoes and bay leaves.

In a large skillet, brown the sausage meat and set aside on paper towels to drain off the excess fat. In the same pan, brown the chicken thighs and either finish cooking in the oven for 20 minutes or cover the skillet and finish cooking on the stovetop. (Always be certain to deglaze the pan with a bit of water and add these drippings to the stockpot to benefit from the rich concentration of flavors left behind from the chicken.)

Combine the meats with the stockpot contents and simmer until the potatoes are tender. Add the black beans and salt and pepper to taste.

What a delicious cold weather offering! Serve this soup with a chunk of good bread and a good football game — and enjoy!

Tortilla Soup

Serves 4

6 tablespoons cooking oil

8 (6 inch) corn tortillas, cut into ¼ inch strips

I onion, chopped

4 cloves garlic, smashed

4 tomatillas, chopped

2 jalapeño peppers, chopped

2 teaspoons cumin

I teaspoon ground coriander

I teaspoon chili powder

¼ teaspoon cayenne pepper

I½ quarts low sodium chicken broth

3 cups canned, crushed tomatoes in thick purée

2 bay leaves

2½ teaspoons salt

¼ cup lightly packed cilantro leaves

3 tablespoons cilantro, chopped (optional)

I¾ pounds cooked chicken breasts, cut into ¾ inch pieces

I avocado, diced into ½ inch pieces

¼ pound Cheddar cheese, grated

Lime wedges for serving

In a large heavy pot, heat oil over medium heat. Add onion, garlic and spices and cook, stirring for 5 minutes. Add broth, tomatoes, jalapeños, tomatillas, bay leaves, salt, cilantro leaves and ⅓ of the tortilla strips. Bring to a simmer. Cook uncovered for 30 minutes. Remove bay leaves. In a blender or food processor, purée soup. Put the soup back in the pot and add the chicken. Bring soup back to a simmer. Stir in avocado. Put remaining strips of tortillas in bowls, top with cheese, and ladle in the soup.

Garnish with chopped cilantro and lime wedges.

Recipe Notes

Recipe Notes

Chicken and Apple Curry Soup

Serves 6

I stick butter

8 green onions, minced

4 celery ribs, diced

$^1/_2$ cup flour

$^3/_4$ cup sherry

$^3/_4$ cup cider

$^3/_4$ cup chicken stock

4 cups milk

2 large green apples, peeled, cored and diced

I tablespoon curry

I tablespoon dried dill weed

2 teaspoons pepper

Salt

In a large heavy saucepan, melt butter over medium heat. Add the green onions, celery, and chicken. Sauté for 10 minutes. Whisk in flour and cook for 3 minutes. Whisk in sherry, cider and stock and cook for 3 minutes until thick. Whisk in milk, add apples and pepper. Simmer until apple is cooked, about 10 minutes. Blend in curry, dill weed and pepper. Add salt to taste.

Hearty Corn Chowder

Serves 8

4 small carrots, peeled and chopped into small pieces

2 ribs celery, sliced

I onion, chopped

2 tablespoons butter

4 cups chicken or vegetable broth

I shallot, chopped

2 teaspoons basil

I teaspoon thyme, chopped

I teaspoon paprika

2 teaspoons minced garlic

I pound potatoes, peeled and chopped

6 cups white corn

2 cups heavy cream (you may use half-and-half)

$\frac{1}{4}$ cup cornstarch

$\frac{1}{4}$ cup dry white wine

Sauté carrots, celery, shallot and onion in butter in a large pot for about 10 minutes. Add broth, basil, thyme, paprika and garlic and bring to a boil. Add potato and corn and bring back to a boil. Add cream and simmer until the vegetables are tender. Separately, mix cornstarch and wine and bring to a boil until smooth. Add a little soup liquid to thin and then stir into soup. Cook until thickened.

Cooked chicken can also be added to this chowder!

Recipe Notes

Recipe Notes

Haddock Chowder

Serves 4

1½ pounds haddock, cut into pieces

3 or 4 white potatoes, cut into small pieces or cubes

1 medium white or yellow onion, finely chopped

1 stick butter or margarine

1½ cups water (or enough to cover potatoes)

1½ cups (more if desired) cream or milk (or a combination of each)

1 can evaporated milk

1 teaspoon dill weed

Ground or cracked pepper

In a large pot and over medium heat, melt butter and add onion. Cook until onion is translucent. Add cut-up potatoes and water and cook until potatoes are tender. Add cut-up haddock and cook through. Add all remaining liquid and salt and pepper to taste. Bring to a near boil and then remove from heat. Float dill weed on top of chowder. Refrigerate overnight to allow flavors to "marry". Heat and serve next day.

One Pan Fish Chowder

Serves 6

4 large potatoes, peeled and cubed

2 pounds of haddock

2 medium onions, thinly sliced

$^1/_3$ cup chopped parsley

4 tablespoons butter

I bay leaf

2 cups boiling water

$^1/_2$ cup white wine

I$^1/_2$ cups cream at room temperature*

Salt and pepper

Parsley or dill for garnish (optional)

Preheat oven to 350°F. In a medium roasting pan, layer half of the potatoes and sprinkle with salt and pepper. Lay whole fish on top. Add onions and celery, then the rest of the potatoes. Dot with pieces of butter. Add bay leaf. Pour boiling water over all and add the white wine. Bake for 1 hour or until potatoes are done. Remove from the oven. Heat the cream and add to the dish, mixing well to break up the fish.

Serve garnished with chopped parsley or dill.

*May substitute low fat evaporated milk for cream.

Recipe Notes

Recipe Notes

Brazilian Fish Chowder

Serves 20

2 jalapeño peppers, chopped

4 garlic cloves, minced

6 scallions, chopped

2 tablespoons butter

6 sweet potatoes, peeled and cubed

8 red potatoes, peeled and cubed

4 cups clam juice (or chicken broth)

6 plum tomatoes, diced

1 can coconut milk

1/4 cup Thai chili garlic sauce

1/4 cup honey

1 pound raw shrimp

2 pounds crabmeat

1 pound scallops

1 pound salmon, poached and chopped

2 cups heavy cream

Melt butter and sauté jalapeño, garlic and scallions. Add the stock and cook the potatoes until almost done. Add the tomatoes, coconut milk, chili sauce, honey and cook on medium-low for 10-15 minutes. Add the seafood, gently cook until done. Before serving, add the cream and heat through.

This recipe is a favorite from Rachel's L'Osteria in Portland, Maine.

Lobster Corn Chowder

Serves 4

4 - 5 strips of bacon

2 large onions, chopped

3 - 4 medium potatoes peeled, diced to ½ inch

32 ounces chicken broth

4 - 5 ears cooked corn, kernels removed

I can (15 ounce) cream style corn

I container (16 ounce) half-and-half

Meat from 2 cooked lobsters

Salt and pepper

Recipe Notes

Sauté the strips of bacon until done; remove from pan. Add the onions and sauté until golden. Add the potatoes and sauté until nearly brown. Add the chicken broth and cook until potatoes are tender. Add the kernels of corn, the can of cream style corn, the half-and-half and lobster and cook until warm only. Season with salt and pepper.

This recipe is a great way to use corn and lobster leftover from a clambake.

Serve with crusty bread and a green salad.

Summer Garden Mussel Bisque

Serves 8

Recipe Notes

2 cups water

1 bottle dry white wine

3 pounds mussels, scrubbed and bearded if necessary

$^1/_2$ cup butter

1 onion, chopped

1 bunch leeks, washed and minced

2 small zucchini, cubed

3 carrots, peeled and minced

4 large cloves of garlic, minced

4 - 6 ripe plum tomatoes, seeded and chopped

2 tablespoons chopped fresh dill

4 tablespoons chopped fresh basil

2 cups light cream

1 cup heavy cream

Salt and pepper to taste

Pour the water and half the wine into large pot. Add the mussels, cover and bring to a boil. Cook over high heat until mussels open, approximately 5 to 10 minutes. Remove from heat and drain in colander, making sure to reserve liquid. Strain liquid through sieve and set aside. Discard any mussels that do not open. When mussels are cool enough to handle, remove meats and set aside.

Melt butter in large stockpot over medium high heat and sauté onion, leek, zucchini, carrots and garlic for five minutes. Reduce heat to low, cover pot and cook for another 20 minutes or until all vegetables are soft. Add the tomatoes and cook uncovered for another 5 minutes. Add remaining wine to mussel liquid. Add to stockpot with vegetables and heat to boiling. Reduce heat and simmer uncovered for 15 minutes.

Stir in herbs, then the light and heavy creams and finally the mussel meats. Season to taste with salt and pepper. Heat until soup is warmed through and then serve immediately.

Can be made a few hours ahead of time up until step of adding herbs and creams.

Serve as main course with crusty bread and a salad, or as first course. A very flavorful soup that is best made with very fresh ingredients.

Mr. Bowker's Oyster Stew

Serves 6

Recipe Notes

6 tablespoons butter, divided

1/2 cup onions, finely minced

1/4 cup flour

2 potatoes, peeled and diced

I quart chicken broth

3/4 teaspoon salt

1/4 teaspoon cayenne pepper

I tablespoon Worcestershire sauce

4 cups shucked oysters, chopped, if desired

2 cups heavy cream

In a large saucepan, over medium heat, sauté the minced onion in 2 tablespoons of butter until onions are translucent, approximately 6 minutes. Add the remaining butter, stir in the flour, and cook for 3 minutes, stirring frequently. Don't let the flour burn. Whisk in the chicken broth and add diced potatoes. Simmer for 15 minutes until the potatoes are cooked. Add salt, cayenne pepper, Worcestershire sauce, oysters and heavy cream. Simmer until the oysters curl. Do not allow to boil.

Chicken and White Bean Chili

Serves 6

1/4 cup olive oil

1 1/3 cups onion, chopped

1 large green bell pepper, chopped

6 garlic cloves, chopped

2 1/4 pounds skinless boneless chicken thighs, cut into 1/2-inch cubes

3 1/2 tablespoons chili powder

3 tablespoons tomato paste

1 1/2 tablespoons ground cumin

1 tablespoon dried oregano

2 cans (15- to 16-ounce) white beans, drained, juices reserved

2 cans (15-ounce) diced tomatoes in juice

1/2 cup fresh cilantro, chopped

Heat oil in heavy large pot over medium-high heat. Add onion, bell pepper, and garlic; sauté until vegetables begin to soften, about 5 minutes. Add chicken; sprinkle with salt and pepper. Sauté until chicken is no longer pink outside, about 5 minutes. Mix in chili powder, tomato paste, cumin, and oregano. Add beans, 1 cup reserved bean juices, and canned tomatoes. Simmer until chicken is cooked through and chili is thickened, about 25 minutes. If chili is too thick, add more bean juices by tablespoonful to thin. Season chili to taste with salt and pepper. Mix in cilantro and serve.

Liz's White Chicken Chili

Serves 4

1½ - 2 pounds boneless, skinless chicken breasts cubed into 1 inch pieces

1 tablespoon oil

1 onion, chopped

1 can (4 ounce) diced green chiles

½ can chicken broth (low-sodium)

1 teaspoon minced garlic

1 teaspoon ground cumin

1 teaspoon dried oregano

¼ teaspoon ground red pepper

2 cans (13 ounce) of cannelini beans, undrained

Heat oil in large skillet and cook chicken approximately 5 minutes. Remove with slotted spoon and set aside in bowl. Cook onion and garlic in pan juices for 2 minutes. Stir in chicken broth, chiles and spices. Simmer uncovered for 30 minutes. Stir in chicken and beans and simmer for another 10 to 15 minutes.

For more "heat" add more spices. Serve with shredded jack cheese and/or sour cream. Great with corn bread!

Recipe Notes

Pumpkin Chili Mexicana

Serves 4

2 tablespoons vegetable oil

¹/₂ cup onion, chopped

I cup red bell pepper, chopped

I clove garlic, finely chopped

I pound ground turkey

I teaspoon cinnamon

2 cans (14.5 ounce) diced tomatoes, undrained

I can (15 ounce) 100% pure pumpkin

I can (15 ounce) tomato sauce

I can (15.25 ounce) kidney beans drained, or black beans or combination

I can (4 ounce) green chiles, diced

¹/₂ cup whole kernel corn

I tablespoon chili powder

I teaspoon ground cumin

I teaspoon salt

¹/₂ teaspoon ground black pepper

Heat the vegetable oil in a large saucepan over medium-high heat. Add the onions, bell pepper and garlic and cook, stirring frequently for 5 to 7 minutes or until tender. Add turkey and cook until browned; drain. Add tomatoes with juice, pumpkin, tomato sauce, beans, chiles, corn, chili powder, cumin, salt and pepper. Bring to a boil. Reduce heat to low. Cover and cook, stirring occasionally for 30 minutes.

Pumpkin lends color and nutrients to this creamy Chili Mexicana.

Great with a cold Mexican beer!

Spicy Southwestern Stew

Serves 6

1 tablespoon vegetable oil

1 large onion, chopped

2 cloves garlic, finely chopped

1 jalapeño pepper, chopped

1½ pounds ground beef

2 tablespoons cumin

1 can (28 ounce) tomatoes

1 can pinto beans, drained and rinsed

1 cup picante sauce

1 large can whole kernel corn

Water

Salt and pepper

In a large pot over medium heat, add oil and sauté onions, garlic and jalapeño pepper for 2 minutes. Add beef and cook until beef is done and there is no red showing. Add cumin and stir. Add tomatoes, beans, picante sauce, corn and salt and pepper. Add water to make the desired consistency. Simmer on low heat for 20 minutes.

Serve with tortilla chips. Also goes well with corn bread.

Recipe Notes

Oven Beef Stew

Serves 4 to 6

Recipe Notes

I onion, chopped

I can (14½ ounce) stewed tomatoes

I can (10½ ounce) mushroom soup

I cup water

¼ cup dry white wine

⅓ cup tapioca

3 or 4 peppercorns

I bay leaf

1½ pounds stew beef, cut into I inch cubes

I pound carrots, cut into I inch cubes

2 large potatoes, cut into I inch cubes

¼ pound mushrooms, sliced

Preheat oven to 350°F. Place all the ingredients into a Dutch oven or covered pan and cook for 3 hours.

Dilled Veal Stew

Serves 8 to 12

Recipe Notes

12 tablespoons butter, divided

3 pounds veal, cut into 1 inch pieces

1/2 cup flour, divided

1/2 teaspoon grated nutmeg

1 1/2 teaspoons salt

1 1/2 teaspoons pepper

3 cups carrots, peeled and sliced

3 cups chopped onion

5 tablespoons chopped fresh dill, divided

3 1/2 cups chicken stock

3/4 cup heavy cream

Melt 8 tablespoons butter in Dutch oven. Add veal and cook, turning without browning. Sprinkle in 3 tablespoons of flour, nutmeg, salt and pepper. Cook over low heat, stirring for approximately 5 minutes without browning the flour.

Add carrots, onions, 3 tablespoon dill and stock to cover meat. Bring to boil, cover, and place in oven at 350°F for 1½ hours.

Remove stew from oven and strain, reserving solids and liquids separately.

Melt remaining butter over medium heat in Dutch oven, sprinkle with remaining flour, whisking constantly for approximately 3 minutes. Whisk in reserved liquids, simmer for approximately 5 minutes, stirring frequently.

Whisk cream, remaining dill and salt and pepper to taste. Return veal and vegetables to the Dutch oven and heat through.

Suggested wine: Chardonnay (buttery)

Spring Fling Jambalaya

Serves 10 to 12

This is a frequently requested favorite at our ski house. I first made it for a spring skiing weekend house party, hence the name. It feeds a crowd and is very filling and flavorful. All you need to serve with it is some good bread, a green salad and red wine. Can make ahead and reheat, and like many casserole type dishes, it is even better the second time around. It also freezes well.

2 tablespoons butter

4 cups chopped onion

I large green bell pepper, chopped

2 bunches sliced scallions

I tablespoon finely minced garlic

3 tablespoons finely minced fresh parsley

I pound lean pork, cut into cubes

I pound ham steak, chopped into cubes

I large or 2 small packages linguica or chorizo sausage, cut into small slices

2 to 3 boneless skinless chicken breasts, cut into bite-size pieces

2 pounds large or jumbo raw shrimp, peeled and deveined

2 cups long grain white rice

3 cups beef stock

1/2 teaspoon freshly ground black pepper

1/2 teaspoon cayenne pepper

I teaspoon chile powder

3 to 4 whole bay leaves, crushed fine

1/2 teaspoon dried thyme

Sauté pork and chicken in butter until cooked through. Set aside in separate dish. Sauté all veggies, including parsley in same pan in remaining liquid. In large stockpot, combine chicken, pork and veggies. Brown ham cubes and sausage slices and add to mixture. Add seasonings and beef stock. Bring to a boil. Add rice and turn down to simmer, covered for 45 minutes, stirring occasionally. If mixture stays too soupy, add rice, if it's too thick just add a little water. Ten minutes before serving, add raw shrimp and mix in thoroughly. The heat of the rest of the mixture should cook the shrimp quickly.

Sides & Salads

Sides & Salads

Vicky's Thanksgiving Onions

Serves 8

2 packages small white onions*

1 package small red onions*

1 large leek

1 tablespoon butter

2 packages soft herb cheese at room temperature

¹/₂ cup cream

3 tablespoons dry white wine or vermouth

Milk, if needed

1 cup grated Gruyère cheese

This delicious family favorite is good any time of the year, but so rich you may only want to serve at the holidays!

Preheat oven to 350°F. Put unpeeled onions in boiling water and boil for 2 minutes, then let rest in boiling water for 5 to 10 minutes. Drain, cool in cold water and peel. Thinly slice leek up to green section and sauté in butter until transparent. While leek is cooking, whisk cheese with cream (add cream slowly) and add white wine. Consistency should be creamy; add milk if you feel it needs to be creamier. Place onions in ovenproof casserole and add cheese mixture. Top with grated Gruyère. Cook uncovered for 45 minutes; check to see if too brown on top. Cover if needed and continue cooking for 15 minutes more.

small net bags are found in the produce department of most supermarkets

Can be prepared ahead of time, but best if served immediately!

Recipe Notes

Maple Glazed Carrots

Serves 6 to 8

2¹/₂ cups water

2 pounds carrots, peeled and sliced into ¹/₂-inch thickness

¹/₃ cup butter, divided

3 teaspoons sugar

I teaspoon kosher salt

3 tablespoons pure maple syrup

2 teaspoons (packed) dark brown sugar

I tablespoon fresh parsley, chopped

Combine water, carrots, 2 tablespoons butter, sugar and salt. Cook carrots until just tender when pierced with a fork. Drain. (May be prepared ahead to this point.) Melt the remaining butter over medium high heat. Add maple syrup and brown sugar and stir until sugar dissolves. Add carrots and cook until carrots are coated and heated through.

Transfer to a bowl and sprinkle with the parsley.

Lentils with Wine-Glazed Vegetables

Serves 8 as a side dish (4 as an entrée)

3 cups water

1½ cups dried lentils (black or French green lentils have the best flavor)

1 teaspoon salt, divided

1 bay leaf

1½ teaspoons olive oil

2 cups onion, chopped

1½ cups celeriac (celery root), peeled and chopped

1 cup parsnip, diced

1 cup carrot, diced

1 tablespoon fresh tarragon, minced or 1 teaspoon dried

1 tablespoon tomato paste

1 garlic clove, minced

²/₃ cup dry red wine

2 teaspoons Dijon mustard

1 tablespoon butter

¼ teaspoon black pepper

Combine water, lentils, ½ teaspoon salt, and bay leaf in medium saucepan; bring to boil. Reduce heat and simmer 25 minutes. Remove from heat; set aside.

Heat olive oil in a medium cast-iron or nonstick skillet over medium-high heat. Add the onion, celeriac, parsnip, carrot, and ½ the tarragon and sauté 10 minutes or until browned. Stir in ½ teaspoon salt, tomato paste and garlic; cook 1 minute. Stir in wine, scraping pan to loosen browned bits. Bring to a boil; cover, reduce heat, and simmer 10 minutes or until vegetables are tender. Stir in mustard. Add lentil mixture, and cook 2 minutes. Remove from heat; discard bay leaf, and stir in butter, the rest of the tarragon, and pepper.

Recipe Notes

Recipe Notes

Traditional Baked Beans

Serves 10 to 12

I pound soldier beans, soaked overnight and drained

I medium onion, whole

$1/2$ pound salt pork, scored

2 tablespoons molasses

2 tablespoons sugar

$1/3$ cup maple syrup

I teaspoon salt

$1/2$ teaspoon black pepper

$1/4$ teaspoon dried mustard

Mix molasses, sugar, maple syrup, salt, pepper and mustard into 2 cup measuring cup. Add boiling water to the 1 cup mark. Mix together. Put beans in a pot with whole onion, salt pork and sauce. Fill bean pot so that beans are covered with water. Cover and bake at 200°F for about 8 hours, adding water if needed.

Great, traditional Maine cookout fare!

Green Beans in Shallot/Sherry Vinaigrette

Serves 8

Recipe Notes

3 strips of bacon

2 shallots, chopped

$^1/_2$ cup sherry vinegar

$^1/_2$ cup olive oil

Salt and pepper

2 pounds green beans

Heat large skillet and add the bacon. Cook until crisp. Drain on paper towel. Cook shallots until transparent in same skillet. Remove and put in a small bowl. Crumble bacon into shallots and add salt and pepper to taste. Mix the vinegar and oil and add to bacon and shallots.

Steam the green beans in same skillet until just tender. Plunge in ice water and drain. Toss with the vinaigrette. Serve warm.

Green beans can be chilled and tossed with the vinaigrette later for a summertime side dish.

Green Beans and Tomato Pesto

Serves 6

1 pound green beans, trimmed

1 clove garlic, crushed

1 teaspoon dried basil

3 tablespoons oil

$^1/_2$ cup walnut halves

$1^1/_2$ cups cherry tomatoes, halved

Cook beans in boiling water 3 to 5 minutes, until crisp, but tender. Drain. (Can be done ahead and finished just before serving.) In a large skillet, sauté garlic and basil in hot oil 1 minute. Add walnuts, stir fry 1 minute. (Again, may be set aside.) Add beans and cherry tomatoes and stir fry for 2 minutes. Serve immediately.

Recipe Notes

Sautéed Mushrooms, Green Beans and Tomatoes with Prosciutto

Serves 6 to 8

I pound cherry tomatoes

$^1/_4$ teaspoon salt

$^1/_4$ teaspoon sugar

$^1/_2$ cup olive oil, divided

6 - 8 garlic cloves, thickly chopped

I pound small mushrooms, halved

I pound green beans

$^1/_4$ tablespoon red pepper flakes

$^1/_4$ pound thinly sliced prosciutto, chopped

$^1/_2$ cup white wine

2 tablespoons parsley, chopped

Grated Parmesan cheese for garnish

Cut tomatoes in half, sprinkle with salt and sugar and set aside. Boil large pot of water, cook beans 7 to 8 minutes. Drain and rinse in cold water. Set aside.

In a skillet cook garlic in ¼ cup olive oil over medium heat until golden, 3 to 5 minutes. Add mushrooms, cook 10 minutes, stirring after 5 minutes. Increase heat to high, add white wine and cook 5 minutes. Pour in a bowl and cover, and set aside.

Heat remaining olive oil to sizzling, add the tomatoes. Reduce the heat and cook 5 minutes. Add beans, prosciutto, red pepper, cook 5 minutes.

Add parsley and combine with the mushrooms.

May be served hot or cold.

Wild Mushroom Strudel

Serves 2

³/₄ pound mixed wild mushrooms (you may substitute a mixture of white button mushrooms)

2 tablespoons olive oil

¹/₂ medium finely chopped onion

I clove garlic, minced

Salt and pepper

¹/₃ cup white wine

¹/₂ teaspoon chopped thyme leaves

¹/₄ pound fresh goat cheese, crumbled

2 tablespoons chopped parsley

4 tablespoons plain dried breadcrumbs, divided

2 sheets phyllo dough

2 tablespoons butter, melted

Clean the mushrooms and slice any large ones into pieces no larger than ¾ inch. In a large skillet over medium heat, heat the oil and add the mushrooms, onion and garlic. Season with salt and pepper and cook, stirring frequently until the mushrooms have released all their liquid and are lightly browned, 10 to 12 minutes.

Add the wine and thyme and cook until the wine has evaporated. Remove from the heat and transfer the mushrooms to a bowl. When the mushrooms are cool, stir in the cheese, parsley and 3 tablespoons of the breadcrumbs. Set aside.

Preheat the oven to 350°F. On a work surface, brush one of the sheets of phyllo with melted butter and dust with the remaining crumbs. Top with the second sheet of phyllo and brush again with butter. Spoon the mushroom mixture down the short end of the phyllo, leaving it about 2 inches from the edge. Fold the dough over the edge and continue rolling, encasing the filling in the phyllo.

Brush the strudel with more butter and carefully transfer to a lightly buttered baking sheet. Bake until golden brown and crispy, about 30 to 35 minutes.

Remove the strudel from the oven and allow to cool 5 minutes. Trim the ends if they are overly brown and frayed. Slice the strudel and serve.

Suggested wine: Malbec

Recipe Notes

Spinach Gratin

Serves 8

4 tablespoons unsalted butter

4 cups onion, diced

1/4 cup flour

1/4 teaspoon nutmeg

1 cup heavy cream

2 cups milk

3 pounds frozen spinach (five 10-ounce packages) thawed and drained

1 cup Parmesan cheese, freshly grated, divided

1/2 teaspoon black pepper

1/2 cup Gruyère cheese, grated

Salt to taste

Preheat oven to 425°F. Melt butter in a heavy sauté pan over medium heat.

Add onions and sauté until translucent, about fifteen minutes. Add flour and nutmeg. Cook, stirring for 2 more minutes; add cream and milk. Cook until thickened. Squeeze as much liquid as possible from the spinach. Add spinach to the sauce. Add ½ cup Parmesan cheese and mix well. Season with salt and pepper. Transfer the spinach to a baking dish and sprinkle remaining Parmesan cheese and the Gruyère cheese on top. (May be made to this point and refrigerated 1 to 2 days ahead.) Bake for 20 minutes until hot and bubbly.

Spinach Soufflé

Serves 4 to 6

I package (10 ounce) frozen
spinach

$^1/_4$ pound **Monterey Jack** cheese,
shredded

$^1/_4$ pound **Cheddar** cheese,
shredded

I pound small curd cottage cheese

2 tablespoons butter

$^1/_4$ cup chopped onion

2 tablespoons flour

3 eggs, slightly beaten

$^1/_4$ teaspoon pepper

Cook and drain the spinach. Set aside. Melt butter and sauté onions.
Add to the spinach. Combine cheeses, flour and pepper. Add eggs
and combine with the spinach. Bake in casserole at 350°F for 55 to
60 minutes.

Baked Tomatoes

Serves 2

2 large tomatoes

4 tablespoons butter

6 heaping tablespoons
breadcrumbs

$^1/_2$ teaspoon Worcestershire sauce

I tablespoon chopped parsley

Cut ⅓ off top of tomatoes. Drain, removing seeds. Melt butter and
mix breadcrumbs, add Worcestershire sauce. Top tomatoes with
bread crumb mixture. Sprinkle with parsley. Place in a baking dish
and bake uncovered, 20 minutes.

Great side dish for brunch OR dinner!

Recipe Notes

Oven Roasted Vegetables

Serves 6

10 small purple or red potatoes, cut in half

1 to 2 cups carrots, peeled and trimmed in large pieces (you may use baby carrots)

1 head of garlic, trim the top

1 small red or white onion, cut into thin wedges

1 tablespoon fresh rosemary or 1 teaspoon dried rosemary

4 sprigs fresh thyme

$^1/_4$ cup olive oil

3 tablespoons lemon juice

1 teaspoon salt

$^1/_2$ teaspoon pepper

1 cup sweet peppers, red or yellow, cut in wedges

In a 9x13-inch roasting pan, combine potatoes, carrots, garlic, onion, rosemary and thyme. Add olive oil and lemon juice. Toss to mix. Sprinkle with salt and pepper. Roast, uncovered, in a 450°F oven for thirty minutes. Remove from oven, add peppers, toss and roast for 10 to 15 minutes more.

You may use any kind of potatoes, add zucchini, cauliflower, squash, parsnips, beets or leeks.

Festive Italian Vegetables

Serves 6

1 pound eggplant, peeled and cubed

1 pound zucchini, sliced

2 medium onions, sliced

1 - 2 garlic cloves, minced

1 green pepper, or red or orange pepper, cubed

1 teaspoon dried oregano

1 teaspoon dried basil

1 jar (16 ounces) marinara sauce

1/2 pound mozzarella cheese, sliced

1/2 pound provolone cheese, sliced

1 pound Italian sausage browned and cut into cubes

May serve as an entrée with crispy garlic bread, fresh green salad and dry red wine.

In a 2½ quart casserole dish layer ½ each of the eggplant, zucchini, onion, pepper and garlic. Sprinkle layer with oregano and basil. Repeat. Pour sauce over vegetables. Cover and bake at 375°F for 45 minutes. Remove from oven and place cooked sausage over vegetables. Arrange mozzarella and provolone cheeses over sausage. Bake 5 to 10 minutes or until cheese is melted.

Pasta Peas

Serves 8 to 10

2 pounds bacon, cut into 1½-inch squares

1 pound smallest shell pasta

8 medium onions, chopped

1 package frozen baby peas, thawed

Parmesan cheese, grated

Cook bacon until crisp, reserving enough fat to sauté onions. Sauté onions until translucent. Cook pasta and drain, but do not rinse. Add onions, bacon, peas, stir and mix. Add grated cheese (as much or as little as you like).

Orzo with Feta Cheese, Peas and Black Olives

Serves 8

I pound orzo

6 - 8 ounces feta cheese, crumbled

3/4 pound frozen baby peas, thawed

1/2 pound pitted and chopped Kalamata black olives

2/3 cup Italian salad dressing

1/2 cup parsley, chopped

Salt and pepper to taste

Cook orzo in boiling water for 10 minutes, drain in colander. Pour orzo in mixing bowl and add Italian dressing, stirring frequently until cool. Add black olives, feta cheese, parsley and stir. Add salt and pepper to taste.

Add more salad dressing if orzo is too thick or looks dry. Capers and/or chopped plum tomatoes may be added for taste and color.

Parsleyed Orzo

Serves 6 to 8

I pound orzo

6 garlic cloves, unpeeled

I cup heavy cream

I cup chicken broth

I cup Parmesan cheese, grated, divided

1¼ cups parsley, chopped, divided

4 tablespoons breadcrumbs

3 tablespoons cold, unsalted butter

Boil orzo with garlic for 10 minutes, drain in colander. Rinse with cold water. Remove garlic, peel and mash with a fork. Whisk garlic with cream, add orzo, stock, ¾ cup Parmesan cheese, and 1 cup parsley. Season with salt and pepper. Pour into buttered 2 quart baking dish. Mix breadcrumbs with remaining Parmesan cheese and parsley. Sprinkle over orzo and dot with butter. Bake 1 hour and 25 minutes in 325°F oven.

Recipe Notes

Recipe Notes

Penne with Gratinée Tomatoes

Serves 8 to 10

$^2/_3$ cup salt packed capers
(**2** small jars)

2 garlic cloves, sliced

$^1/_3$ cup basil leaves

16 large plum tomatoes, cut half lengthwise, seeded and cored.

$^1/_2$ cup olive oil

$^1/_2$ cup dry breadcrumbs

Sea salt

I pound penne

Preheat oven to 350°F and foil 2 cookie sheets. Soak capers in three changes of water and dry. Combine with garlic and basil and chop until fine on a cutting board. Arrange tomatoes, cut side up on cookie sheets. Put caper mixture on each and drizzle with olive oil. Sprinkle breadcrumbs on tomatoes and salt. Bake 1 hour and 15 minutes.

Cook penne, drain and rinse. Toss tomato mixture with penne and serve.

Summer Spaghetti

Serves 4 to 5

8 large fresh tomatoes

$^1/_2$ - I cup chopped fresh basil

4 cloves garlic, crushed

I pound fresh mozzarella cheese, diced or shredded

I$^1/_2$ cups virgin olive oil

I pound pasta, thin spaghetti like capellini or angel hair

Parmesan cheese, grated or shredded

Salt and pepper, to taste

Peel, seed and chop tomatoes. In a large bowl combine tomatoes, mozzarella cheese, basil, garlic and olive oil. Toss gently. Cover and let mixture stand at room temperature for at least 30 minutes. Cook and drain pasta. Toss lightly with the tomato mixture. Season with salt and freshly ground pepper to taste. Top with Parmesan cheese. Serve immediately.

Recipe Notes

Sesame Noodles

Serves 8 to 12

A good summer evening meal might include this dish with spicy marinated pork loin and Asian salad. You add the company!

1 pound linguini or Chinese style noodles

3½ tablespoons dark soy sauce

3½ tablespoons sesame oil

1½ tablespoons black or red vinegar

2 tablespoons sugar

2 teaspoons kosher salt

2 tablespoons peanut butter

1 bunch scallions, sliced

Cook linguini until al dente. While pasta is cooking, blend together in food processor soy sauce, sesame oil, vinegar, sugar, salt and peanut butter. Drain pasta and toss well with the soy/peanut dressing. Top with scallions. Serve warm or room temperature.

Beach Potatoes

Serves 4 to 6

3 white potatoes, peeled and thinly sliced

3 sweet potatoes, thinly sliced

3 white onions, thinly sliced

Olive oil

Salt and pepper

Coat 9x13-inch glass pan with olive oil, salt and pepper. Layer potatoes and onions. Drizzle with olive oil. Bake at 375°F for 45 minutes.

May be baked in individual foil packets on a grill.

Easy Oven Roast Potatoes

Serves 4 to 6

2 - 3 pounds red potatoes

2 tablespoons olive oil

Salt and pepper

Paprika

Chop potatoes into 1 to 2 inch quarters or pieces (leave skin on). Toss with olive oil. Season to taste with salt and pepper. Spread on cookie sheet. Sprinkle with paprika. Roast for 1 hour, at half hour mark, use spatula to flip potatoes over.

Recipe Notes

Horseradish Mashed Potatoes with Caramelized Onions

Serves 6 to 8

6 tablespoons butter (or use half the amount of butter and spray onions with vegetable cooking spray)

2¹/₂ pounds yellow or white onions, thinly sliced

3 tablespoons balsamic vinegar

2 teaspoons fresh thyme, chopped or use ¹/₄ teaspoon dried thyme

3¹/₂ pounds russet potatoes, peeled, cut into pieces

¹/₄ cup white horseradish (hot **Kosher** horseradish is recommended)

6 - 8 tablespoons milk

Melt ¼ cup butter in a large skillet over medium heat. Add onions, sauté until deep golden, about 30 minutes. Add vinegar and thyme, reduce heat. Continue to sauté 4-5 minutes. Season with salt and pepper.

Meanwhile, cook potatoes in boiling water until tender, approximately 20 minutes. Drain. Add milk (more if necessary to get the right consistency for mashed potatoes) and horseradish and beat with an electric mixer until smooth. Transfer potatoes to a greased oblong casserole. Cover with caramelized onions. Cover and refrigerate until ready to reheat.

Bring to room temperature and heat at 350°F for approximately 15-20 minutes.

Potato Casserole

Serves 10 to 12

2 pound bag frozen hash browns

I pound sour cream

I can cream of chicken soup

8 ounces sharp Cheddar cheese, shredded

I cup finely diced onion

I stick butter, melted

Salt, pepper and garlic powder to taste

Mix ingredients in large bowl and spread in greased 9x13-inch casserole. Bake at 350°F for 1 hour.

So simple you can mix it in the casserole, refrigerate and put in oven an hour before you serve your guests!

Potato Cheese Pie

Serves 6 to 8

3 pounds potatoes (Maine russets)

3 tablespoons butter

$^1/_2$ cup milk

$^1/_2$ cup Parmesan cheese, grated

2 eggs, beaten

Salt, pepper, breadcrumbs

Mozzarella cheese, thinly sliced

Peel and boil potatoes. Drain and mash potatoes, adding butter, milk, grated cheese, eggs, salt and pepper. Beat until creamy and light. Butter 8-inch pie plate and sprinkle breadcrumbs on bottom. Put ½ potato mixture and cover with mozzarella cheese slices. Top with remaining potatoes. Sprinkle breadcrumbs and dot with butter. Bake at 375°F until golden brown and crusty.

Recipe Notes

Irish Potatoes

Serves 8 to 10

10 medium potatoes, peeled, boiled, and mashed.

1 stick butter

8 ounces sour cream

1 package (8 ounce) cream cheese

$1/4$ cup chives, chopped

Mix well and refrigerate for 24 hours. Turn into a buttered casserole and bake at 350°F for 30 minutes.

Tabbouleh

Serves 6

$1^1/2$ cups bulgur wheat

$1^1/2$ cups boiling water

2 lemons, juiced

2 cloves garlic, minced

1 bunch of fresh mint, chopped

3 bunches parsley, chopped

4 scallions, chopped

2 cups cherry tomatoes, halved

1 cucumber, peeled, seeded and diced

Salt and pepper to taste

Place bulgur wheat in a bowl and pour the boiling water over the wheat and let soak for 30 to 45 minutes. Squeeze out any excess water. Mix lemon juice, garlic, chopped herbs, scallions, tomatoes, cucumbers and toss. Add salt and pepper to taste. Add more lemon juice if desired.

May be prepared ahead of time.

Creamy Polenta

Serves 6 to 8

¼ cup olive oil

1 cup chopped onion

2 garlic cloves, minced

1½ teaspoons fresh thyme, or ¼ teaspoon dried

3 cups low-salt chicken broth

2 cups whole milk

1½ cups quick cooking polenta

1 cup Parmesan or pecorino cheese, coarsely grated or ½ cup finely grated

In a medium heated saucepan, add olive oil and onion. Sauté until the onions are translucent, add the garlic and cook for 1 to 2 minutes more. Add the thyme and cook for 1 minute. Pour in the chicken broth and milk and heat until nearly boiling. Add the polenta, stirring constantly as the polenta thickens, about 3 to 4 minutes if using quick cooking polenta, 10 to 15 minutes if using cornmeal. When the polenta has thickened, remove from heat and stir in cheese, salt and pepper. Pour into a buttered or oiled 9x13-inch pan and cover with saran wrap. Pat the surface smooth, refrigerate when cooled. Let polenta set for 2 hours. 15 minutes before serving, remove polenta from the refrigerator and cut into 12 pieces. Lightly dust with flour and sauté in a skillet over medium heat for 5 minutes, turn and cook 5 more minutes, until heated thoroughly. Serve immediately.

May be made several days ahead and re-heated.

Rice Pilaf with Ginger

Serves 6

4½ tablespoons olive oil, divided

2 tablespoons butter

I piece ginger (approximately 1½ inches by 3 inches) peeled and cut into tiny matchsticks

2 cups basmati rice

2 cups water

2 cups low salt chicken broth

4 to 6 medium shallots, peeled, sliced crosswise into thin rings

I bunch of asparagus (approximately I pound) with ends trimmed and sliced diagonally into thirds

I box tiny frozen peas

Salt and pepper to taste

In a large heavy saucepan over high heat, heat 1½ tablespoons of the oil. When hot, melt the butter. Add ginger matchsticks (they'll sizzle), then lower the heat to medium and cook the ginger for 2 minutes or until it has swollen slightly and turned golden brown at the edges. Reduce heat to medium-high and add the rice. Stir the rice to coat it with oil and continue cooking for 3 to 4 minutes or until the rice turns opaque. Turn up the heat, add the water and stock and a pinch of salt. Bring to a low boil, lower the heat immediately, cover and cook the rice over medium-low heat for 20 to 25 minutes or until the rice is done. Meanwhile, in a large skillet, heat the remaining 3 tablespoons of olive oil, add the shallots and turn the heat to medium. Cook the shallots for 7 to 8 minutes, stirring frequently to prevent burning. Add asparagus and cook until tender but not overcooked. Add the peas and stir 2 minutes just to warm them through. Remove vegetables from heat. When rice is cooked, stir in vegetables, add salt and pepper to taste and serve at once.

This is a very flavorful rice pilaf dish with a nice twist added from the ginger. It reads longer and more complicated than it really is. Can be doubled easily and reheats well.

Mediterranean Spinach Salad

Serves 4 to 6

12 ounces fresh spinach, rinsed and spun dry

1 small cucumber, peeled, seeded and sliced

1 small red onion, thinly sliced

1½ cups marinated sun-dried tomatoes, drained and chopped

12 ounces feta cheese, crumbled

½ cup Kalamata olives, pitted

Place the spinach in a large salad bowl suitable for serving. Arrange the cucumber, onions, sun-dried tomatoes, black olives, and feta cheese over the top

DRESSING

⅔ cup red wine vinegar

2 fresh garlic cloves, minced

2 teaspoons dried Italian herb blend

2 teaspoons sugar

½ cup extra virgin olive oil

½ cup fresh basil leaves, chopped

Salt and pepper to taste

Whisk together the vinegar, herbs and sugar. Slowly whisk the oil into the mixture in a stream. Continue to whisk until slightly thickened. Season with salt and pepper. Stir in basil. Drizzle over the spinach, vegetables and cheese. Toss and serve.

You may add cooked and chilled shrimp, crab or lobster or grilled chicken for a salad that is a meal.

Recipe Notes

Recipe Notes

Fast and Easy Antipasto Salad

Serves 10 to 12

I large head Romaine lettuce, chopped

I package cherry tomatoes, halved

I can artichoke hearts, drained and quartered

I tub marinated mini mozzarella

I cup pitted Kalamata olives

I cup pepperoncini, halved with stems removed

I package sliced pepperoni

I bottle Italian salad dressing

Combine all ingredients and toss with dressing to your liking. Other optional add-ins are chopped scallions, garbanzo beans, or any other ingredient you like.

This is great for a crowd, and my family loves it as an accompaniment to takeout pizza.

Salad Ultimate

Serves 8 to 10

I bunch red leaf lettuce

2 cups Romaine lettuce, chopped

2 cups iceberg lettuce, torn

I cucumber, peeled, seeded and sliced

I cup tomatoes, chopped

I cup red bell pepper, chopped

I cup celery, chopped

$^1/_2$ cup radish, chopped

I cup snow peas

I cup carrots, peeled and sliced

$^1/_2$ cup craisins

$^1/_2$ cup walnuts, chopped

I cup croutons

I cup pepper jack cheese, shredded

Place the lettuce mixture in a serving bowl and mix. Top with all the remaining ingredients. Serve with your favorite red wine vinaigrette salad dressing.

This salad is very colorful and would be perfect for a summer buffet.

Asian Salad

Serves 6

Recipe Notes

1 head Napa cabbage, chopped finely

1 bunch scallions, chopped

½ cup sesame seeds

2 packages Ramen noodles, broken into 1-inch pieces

3 tablespoons butter

Combine the cabbage and scallions together and refrigerate. Sauté the sesame seeds and ramen noodles (discard seasoning package) in melted butter until slightly brown. Set aside.

DRESSING

⅓ cup salad oil

⅓ cup sugar

⅓ cup white or rice vinegar

2½ tablespoons soy sauce

1 tablespoon sesame oil

Whisk salad oil, sugar, vinegar, soy sauce and sesame oil together, making sure all the sugar is thoroughly blended in the dressing, and set aside. At the last minute before serving, combine the cabbage-scallion mixture, the ramen noodle-sesame seed mixture, and dressing.

Add 1 teaspoon of Accent to dressing mixture and/or add ½ cup toasted slivered almonds.

Green Bean and Tomato Salad

Serves 6

1¹/₂ pounds fresh green beans

1 package grape tomatoes, halved

4 ounces feta cheese, crumbled

³/₄ cup fresh basil, chopped

2 garlic cloves, crushed

2 - 3 tablespoons good olive oil

Cut the green beans into 1-inch pieces and boil for 3 to 4 minutes, then immerse in a bowl of ice water. Put salt and pepper in the bottom of a wooden serving bowl and crush the garlic with the salt and pepper. Add the chilled, drained green beans, tomatoes, basil and feta cheese. Toss well to serve.

This salad can also be made using asparagus in place of the green beans. Try tossing it with hot pasta for a main dish.

Recipe Notes

Recipe Notes

Mixed Greens with Sautéed Goat Cheese Rounds

Serves 6

I log (II ounce) plain or herbed goat cheese

2 extra large egg whites, beaten

I tablespoon fresh white breadcrumbs

Fresh mixed greens for 6

Olive oil and unsalted butter for frying

Slice the goat cheese into 12 (½ inch) slices. (The easiest way to slice goat cheese is to use a length of dental floss.) Dip each slice into the beaten egg whites, then the breadcrumbs, being sure the cheese is thoroughly coated. Place the slices on a parchment lined cookie sheet and chill them for at least 15 minutes.

DRESSING

2 tablespoons cider vinegar

2 tablespoons champagne vinegar

Pinch of sugar

½ teaspoon kosher salt

¼ teaspoon fresh ground pepper

I extra large egg yolk

I cup olive oil

Place the vinegars, sugar, salt, pepper and egg yolk in the food processor and blend for 1 minute. With the motor running, slowly pour the olive oil through the feed tube until the vinaigrette is thickened.

Toss the salad greens with enough dressing to moisten, then divide among 6 plates. Mix 1 tablespoon oil and 1 tablespoon butter in sauté pan over medium high heat until just smoking. Add more oil if needed. Cook the goat cheese rounds quickly on both sides until browned but not melted. Top two on each salad and serve immediately.

Three Pea Salad with Mint

Serves 10 to 12

1 large package frozen peas or 3 cups fresh shelled

8 ounces fresh snow peas, trimmed

8 ounces sugar snap peas, trimmed

1 large bunch fresh mint

$^1/_2$ cup sour cream

$^1/_2$ cup mayonnaise

8 slices crisp cooked bacon, crumbled

Salt and pepper to taste

Steam frozen peas and drain. Blanch snow peas and snap peas in boiling water until bright green and crisp, approximately 1 minute. Drain and rinse both pans of peas with cold water. Set aside.

Finely chop mint, reserving a few leaves for garnish. Cut snow and snap peas into julienne strips, again reserving a few for garnish. Combine all 3 peas into large bowl.

Mix sour cream and mayonnaise together and fold into pea mixture. Season to taste with salt and pepper. Cover and refrigerate until cold.

To serve, sprinkle bacon on top and garnish with reserved peas and mint leaves.

This is a great side dish on a hot summer day and goes well with grilled lamb or salmon. A family favorite on the Fourth of July when we serve the traditional New England fare of salmon and peas.

Mandarin Salad

Serves 6

To test avocados for ripeness, very gently press the fruit. If it yields to pressure, it is ripe. Avocados bruise easily and bruises will result in dark rot under the skin. Plan several days ahead to ripen the fruit at room temperature. The flesh oxidizes quickly when exposed to air. After cutting the avocado, brush the flesh with lemon or lime juice. Wrap any unused flesh tightly in plastic wrap and refrigerate. Should the flesh develop dark spots, just cut the spots out.

I head Bibb lettuce, torn into bite-sized pieces

I package (**6** ounce) baby spinach

$^1/_2$ red onion, chopped

I large can Mandarin oranges, drained

I avocado, chopped

DRESSING

$^2/_3$ cup orange marmalade

I teaspoon dry mustard

I teaspoon salt

I teaspoon onion, grated

$^1/_3$ cup white vinegar

I cup vegetable oil

In a large salad bowl, combine the greens and top with mandarin oranges and onion. Whisk together the ingredients for the dressing in a small bowl. Toss the salad, oranges, avocado and onion together, using half the dressing. Serve the other half of the dressing on the side.

Arugula, Blue Cheese and Pear Salad

Serves 6

I package of arugula

5 ounces blue cheese, crumbled
into 1-inch pieces

2 pears, peeled, cored and sliced
into thin wedges

$^1/_2$ cup chopped walnuts

DRESSING

I tablespoon course grained Dijon
mustard

2 tablespoons balsamic vinegar

5 tablespoons good olive oil

Rinse and dry arugula and distribute onto 6 salad plates. Whisk together the ingredients for the dressing by placing them into a small, covered jar. Shake until blended. Top each plate of arugula with the portion of the pear and cheese. Sprinkle walnuts over the top. Just before serving, drizzle with dressing.

Recipe Notes

Recipe Notes

Pasta Salad with Sun-Dried Tomatoes, Olives and Mozzarella Cheese

Serves 6

6 tablespoons olive oil

$1/2$ cup oil packed sun-dried tomatoes, drained and chopped

$1/4$ cup red wine vinegar

$1/2$ cup capers, drained

1 - 2 garlic cloves, minced

1 pound fusilli pasta

3 plum tomatoes, chopped

8 - 10 ounces fresh mozzarella, cut into $1/2$-inch pieces

1 cup fresh chopped basil

1 cup fresh Parmesan cheese, grated

$1/2$ cup pitted and chopped Kalamata black olives

Blend together the olive oil, sun-dried tomatoes, red wine vinegar, capers and garlic and then set aside. Cook the pasta until just tender but firm, and drain. Transfer to a large bowl. Add the dressing immediately and mix to coat the pasta. Cool the mixture. Add the tomatoes, mozzarella, basil, Parmesan cheese and olives. Toss together and serve at room temperature.

Waldorf Pasta Salad

Serves 6

I box farfalle (bowtie) pasta

I - 2 green apples, peeled, cored, chopped

$^1/_2$ cup celery, chopped

$^1/_2$ cup walnuts, chopped

$^1/_2$ cup dates, chopped

$^1/_2$ cup light mayonnaise

I cup of lemon yoghurt

Cook pasta, drain and rinse with cold water. Combine in a bowl, pasta, apples, celery, walnuts and dates. In a smaller bowl, thoroughly blend mayonnaise and yoghurt. Add to pasta mixture. Chill before serving.

Dad's Cole Slaw

Serves 10 to 12

I medium/large cabbage, cored and shredded

2 - 3 carrots, peeled and grated

2 tablespoons onion, chopped fine

2 cups mayonnaise

$^3/_4$ cup sugar

$^1/_4$ cup Dijon mustard

$^1/_4$ cup cider vinegar

$^1/_2$ teaspoon celery seed

I teaspoon salt

$^1/_4$ teaspoon white pepper

Prepare vegetables and place in large bowl, set aside. Combine well all other ingredients in another bowl. Add to vegetables and toss well. Cover and refrigerate for at least 4 hours before serving.

Can be made the night before.

A classic cole slaw recipe that my dad always makes. Great summertime side dish!

Recipe Notes

Recipe Notes

Roasted Potato Salad with Balsamic Vinaigrette

Serves 6 to 8

2 pounds Yukon gold potatoes

$^{1}/_{4}$ cup good olive oil

I teaspoon salt

$^{1}/_{4}$ teaspoon pepper

I fennel bulb

$^{1}/_{2}$ teaspoon thyme

3 tablespoons balsamic vinegar

2 tablespoons coarse grain mustard

$^{1}/_{4}$ cup extra virgin olive oil

I tablespoon fennel seeds, roasted

Preheat oven to 400°F. In a bowl, combine the potatoes with olive oil, salt and pepper. Toss to coat the potatoes; spread on a baking sheet and roast the potatoes until they are tender on the inside and crisp on the outside (about 45 minutes). Let cool for 10 minutes. While the potatoes are roasting, shave the washed fennel bulb using a mandolin or the slicing side of a box grater. Mix the vinaigrette by whisking the thyme, vinegar, mustard and oil together. Add the fennel shavings to the roasted potatoes and toss with the vinaigrette. Serve warm or chilled.

Brown Rice Salad with Balsamic Vinaigrette

Serves 8

I cup uncooked brown rice

2 cups water

I teaspoon kosher salt

3 tablespoons balsamic vinegar

2 tablespoons coarse grain mustard

$\frac{1}{4}$ cup good olive oil

$\frac{1}{2}$ teaspoon black pepper

I cup cherry tomatoes, halved

$\frac{1}{2}$ cup pitted Kalamata olive

$\frac{1}{2}$ cup yellow pepper, diced

$\frac{1}{2}$ cup basil, chopped

In a saucepan bring water and salt to a boil. Stir in rice, cover and reduce heat to low. Simmer 45-60 minutes or until rice is done. In a small bowl, combine vinegar, mustard, olive oil and pepper. Mix thoroughly then pour over rice while the rice is still warm. Add tomatoes, olives, pepper and basil just before serving. Serve chilled or at room temperature.

Recipe Notes

Recipe Notes

Curried Rice Salad

Serves 6

1 tablespoon olive oil

1 teaspoon curry powder

1 can (13³/₄ ounce) chicken broth

1 cup celery, chopped

1 cup uncooked brown rice

¹/₂ cup water

¹/₂ cup slivered almonds, toasted

¹/₃ cup mayonnaise

¹/₄ cup parsley, chopped

1 can artichoke hearts, drained (optional)

¹/₂ cup cherry tomatoes, halved (optional)

In a saucepan, heat oil. Add curry powder; heat gently for 1 minute. Add broth, celery, rice and water. Heat to boiling, lower heat, cover and simmer for 20 to 25 minutes or until liquid is absorbed. Chill 6 hours or overnight. Stir in almonds and mayonnaise. You may add a can of drained quartered artichoke hearts. Garnish with halved cherry tomatoes and parsley.

Curry Chicken Salad

1 can (8 ounce) pineapple chunks

²/₃ cup light mayonnaise

1 tablespoon Dijon mustard

1¹/₂ teaspoons curry powder

¹/₂ cup celery, chopped

Salt to taste

2 tablespoons green onions, thinly sliced

4 cups chicken, cooked and chopped into bite size pieces

¹/₃ cup slivered almonds, toasted

¹/₃ cup raisins

Combine 2 tablespoons of the juice from the canned pineapple with mayonnaise, mustard, curry and salt. Place the chicken in a bowl and mix with the celery, green onions, almonds, drained pineapple chunks and raisins. Combine the flavored mayonnaise with the chicken mixture. Refrigerate until serving.

Sushi Shrimp Salad

Serves 8 to 12

4 cups cooled jasmine rice

2 cucumbers, peeled, seeded and diced

1 package (10 ounce) frozen peas or 1 cup cooked fresh peas

1 bunch sliced scallions

1 bunch thinly sliced red radishes

1 pound cooked, peeled and deveined large (31 to 35 count) shrimp

DRESSING

$^1/_2$ cup seasoned rice vinegar

2 tablespoons minced fresh ginger

2 tablespoons prepared horseradish

2 tablespoons Asian sesame oil

In small bowl, whisk together dressing ingredients and set aside. In large bowl, combine cooked rice, cucumbers, radishes, onions and dressing. Gently mix in shrimp. Just before serving, toss with dressing.

Unusual side dish or salad that gets rave reviews every time! Nice on a very hot day.

Lobster Salad Parfait

Serves 4 to 8

This is a gorgeous appetizer or salad course. It is refreshing in the summer but also very festive at the holidays! I have used it successfully year round and guests always love it.

I pound cooked lobster meat

I jar fresh pink grapefruit sections

I tablespoon minced shallots

I¹/₄ teaspoons Dijon mustard

2 tablespoons white wine vinegar

I tablespoon freshly chopped lemon basil or regular basil

Coarse salt and freshly ground pepper

¹/₄ cup virgin olive oil

2 avocados, peeled and pitted

I can hearts of palm, cut in ¹/₂-inch rounds

I large head Boston or butter lettuce

Drain the grapefruit, reserving ½ cup for the dressing. Place shallots, mustard, vinegar, grapefruit juice, and basil in a bowl; season with salt and pepper. Whisk to combine. Gradually whisk in olive oil. Slice avocados into ½-inch wedges. Add lobster, grapefruit sections and hearts of palm. Line clear glass bowls or balloon wine glasses with large lettuce leaves. Tear remaining lettuce into bite size pieces and add to lobster mixture. Drizzle with dressing and toss. Fill lettuce lined bowls with mixture.

Entrees

Entrées

Filet Mignon with Port Mustard Sauce

Recipe Notes

Serves 4

2 tablespoons olive oil

4 (5 to 6 ounce) filets mignon (about 1¹/₂ inches thick)

3 tablespoons shallot, minced

¹/₃ cup Port

²/₃ cup dry red wine

I cup beef broth

1¹/₂ teaspoons Dijon mustard

I tablespoon unsalted butter, softened

I tablespoon flour

In heavy skillet, heat oil over moderately high heat until hot but not smoking. Season the filets with salt and pepper, and cook for 2 minutes on each side. Continue to sauté the filets, turning them on both sides and edges for 4-6 more minutes for medium rare. When meat is cooked to your desire, remove from skillet, cover loosely with foil.

In the fat remaining in the skillet, sauté the shallot over moderately low heat until softened. Add the Port and wine and boil mixture until reduced by half. Add the broth, boil mixture until this is reduced by half. Remove from heat and strain through fine sieve into small saucepan.

Knead together butter and flour.

Whisk the mustard into the saucepan and bring the mixture to a boil. Add the butter and flour mixture, a little at a time, whisking until the sauce is smooth. Simmer the sauce, whisking occasionally for about 2 minutes. Season with salt and pepper.

To plate, either slice the filets into ¼ thick slices, dividing the slices among 4 plates and spoon the sauce over the filets or serve each person their uncut filet, passing the sauce for individual serving.

Suggested wine: Cabernet Sauvignon

Skirt Steak with Onion Marmalade

Serves 4

If you don't want to make the marmalade, try Maine's Stonewall Kitchen's Roasted Garlic Onion Jam!

I cup sugar, divided

I cup dry red wine

I large red onion, thinly sliced

¼ cup red wine vinegar

¼ cup plus 2 tablespoons extra-virgin olive oil, divided

I large Spanish onion, finely chopped

4 garlic cloves, 2 thinly sliced, 2 minced

I jar (8-ounce) roasted red peppers, drained (about I cup)

2 tablespoons sherry vinegar

Salt and pepper

½ teaspoon cayenne pepper

½ teaspoon cumin

I½ pounds skirt steak, cut crosswise into 4 pieces

To prepare the marmalade, combine in a medium saucepan ½ cup of the sugar with the wine and bring to a boil, stirring to dissolve the sugar. Add the red onion, cover and cook over high heat, stirring occasionally, until softened, about 5 minutes. Drain the onion slices and discard the liquid. Return the onion to the pan. Add the remaining ½ cup of sugar and the red wine vinegar and cook over moderate heat, stirring occasionally, until syrupy, about 6 minutes longer.

Meanwhile prepare the red pepper sauce in a large skillet by heating 2 tablespoons of the olive oil until shimmering. Add the Spanish onion and cook over moderately high heat, stirring, until softened, about 5 minutes. Add the sliced garlic and roasted red peppers and cook over moderate heat until the garlic is softened, about 5 minutes. Add the sherry vinegar. Scrape the mixture into a food processor and purée until fairly smooth. Season the red pepper sauce with salt and pepper and transfer to a bowl. Rinse out the skillet and pat dry.

Heat the skillet until hot, but not smoking. In a small bowl, combine the remaining ¼ cup of olive oil with the minced garlic, cayenne and cumin. Rub the mixture over the steaks and season with salt. Add

Skirt Steak with Onion Marmalade — continued

the steaks to the skillet and cook them over high heat, turning once, until they are medium-rare, about 5 minutes.

Transfer the steaks to plates and serve with the onion marmalade and red pepper sauce.

Suggested wine: Zinfandel

Huxley Flank Steak Marinade

Serves 4 to 6

3 cloves garlic, pressed

$^1/_3$ cup soy sauce

2 tablespoons tomato paste

2 tablespoons peanut oil

I teaspoon cracked black pepper

I teaspoon oregano

$1^3/_4$ pound flank steak

Combine marinade. Mix. Coat flank steak. Let sit at room temperature for 1 hour. Grill one side, then the other, over hot coals. Slice thinly, cooked ends first.

Suggested wine: Zinfandel

Another marinade for beef or chicken

$^1/_2$ cup canola oil

$^1/_3$ cup soy sauce

$^1/_4$ cup lemon juice

2 tablespoons prepared yellow mustard

2 tablespoons Worcestershire sauce

I clove garlic, minced

I teaspoon black pepper

Whisk ingredients together. Pour in 1 gallon freezer bag and add meat. How much meat you use and how long you marinate will determine strength of flavor.

Bacon Wrapped Tips of Tenderloin

Serves 4

Recipe Notes

1½ pounds tenderloin beef tips

½ pound smoked bacon

4 cups Swiss chard, chopped and packed

2 tablespoons olive oil

2 cups red wine

1 cup small white beans, cooked

½ cup thickened beef broth

¼ cup porcini mushrooms, chopped

¼ cup sun-dried tomatoes (no oil), chopped

1 teaspoon garlic, chopped

1 teaspoon brown sugar

1 bay leaf

3 tablespoons onion, chopped

Salt and pepper to taste

Heat olive oil in saucepan over medium-low heat and cook chopped onions until softened, but not brown. Add red wine, white beans, beef broth, mushrooms, sun-dried tomatoes, garlic, brown sugar, bay leaf and salt and pepper. Bring to simmer and cook for 10 minutes. Keep warm.

Wrap tenderloin tips with the uncooked smoked bacon. Season with salt and pepper. Sear the tips in a hot skillet until bacon has browned. Remove tips from the skillet and cook in 400°F oven for 8-14 minutes, depending on how well done you like your meat.

In skillet over medium-high heat, wilt the Swiss chard in olive oil and season with salt and pepper.

To plate, place Swiss chard in center of plate, arranging meat tips around the plate. Top with the sauce.

Suggested wine: Cabernet Sauvignon

Mom's Best Brisket

Serves 10

6 pounds single brisket, or
2 smaller cuts

2 large onions sliced

2 cloves garlic, minced

¾ cup brown sugar

½ cup cider vinegar

I cup ketchup

I cup water

I tablespoon salt

Freshly ground pepper

Oil or spray for browning meat

This was my mother's most requested dinner. The great thing about this recipe is that it MUST be made at least the day ahead for the flavors to improve. Simply reheat in the oven at 350°F. Perfect for stress-free entertaining.

Place brisket in a heavy skillet or large Dutch oven and brown on all sides. If using two smaller cuts, brown one at a time. Take brisket out and put on a platter. Brown onions and garlic. Add remaining ingredients and put brisket back into the pot.

You can either cook, covered, on low flame for 2 to 3 hours, or put in the oven covered at 325°F for the same amount of time. Check at the 2 hour mark. If the meat is tender but not falling apart, take the brisket out of the pot and put on a large cutting board. This will be a bit messy, but worth it. Slice the meat, while it is not quite done, across the grain into ½ to ¾-inch slices. Carefully place the slices back into the pot, cover and cook until so tender that you cut the brisket with a fork, ½ to 1 hour longer.

You can either plate up the brisket or you can place in a 2-inch deep baking/serving dish with the delicious gravy and serve family style. Any extra can be stored and reheated in the baking dish. This recipe can be frozen easily and tastes just as delicious thawed and reheated.

Serve with mashed potatoes or couscous and a green salad.

Suggested wine: Carmanere

Beef Stroganoff

Serves 8

Recipe Notes

2¹/₂ pounds beef tenderloin, cut into ¹/₂-inch thick strips

I teaspoon paprika

Salt and pepper to taste

6 tablespoons unsalted butter, divided

2 tablespoons olive oil

2¹/₂ cups mushrooms, sliced

¹/₂ cup shallots, chopped

3 tablespoons flour

¹/₂ cup dry white wine

I cup beef stock

³/₄ cup sour cream

Sprinkle the beef with the paprika, salt and pepper. In large sauté pan, melt half of the butter and olive oil over medium high heat and brown meat for about 1 minute. Do not crowd the meat strips; you want to sear the meat, not boil it. Set the meat aside.

Add the remaining butter to the pan and sauté the mushrooms until the liquid has been rendered, continue to cook for 5 minutes. Add the shallots and sauté until the shallots are soft and the mushrooms begin to brown.

Sprinkle the flour over the mushrooms and stir until mixed. Add the wine, stirring and boil for 1 minute. Add the stock, reduce the heat and simmer until slightly thickened or for about 10 minutes. Remove from the heat, stir in the sour cream. Add the meat and any accumulated juices. Reduce the heat to low and cook for a few minutes to warm the heat. Do not boil or the sour cream will curdle.

Correct the seasoning and serve over egg noodles.

Suggested wine: Shiraz

Mexican Casserole

Serves 4 to 6

I pound ground beef

8 ounce jar mild salsa

$\frac{1}{2}$ cup sour cream

2 ounces pimientos

I package (10 ounce) corn tortillas

I cup Cheddar cheese, shredded

Brown and drain ground beef. Mix beef, salsa, sour cream, and pimientos. Cut tortillas into strips and cover an 8 x 8-inch casserole dish with half of the strips. Add half of the ground beef mixture. Repeat layers and top with 1 cup shredded cheese. Bake in 350°F oven about 30 minutes.

Cris's Italian Style Leg of Lamb

Serves 6

I small leg of lamb

I whole head of garlic

$\frac{1}{4}$ pound prosciutto, sliced thin

Fresh rosemary

Salt and pepper

2 tablespoons Parmesan cheese, finely grated

Cut little slits all around the surface of the leg of lamb at regular intervals. Break apart garlic head, cutting larger sections of garlic into smaller pieces. Roll small pieces of prosciutto with 3-4 rosemary leaves. Alternating, insert garlic pieces and then prosciutto/rosemary pieces into slits in the lamb. Let rest at room temperature at least 2 hours or preferably overnight.

Bake at 400°F for 12 minutes per pound. This will result in a rare leg of lamb. If you prefer, cook longer for desired doneness. When lamb is approximately ¾ done, sprinkle with grated cheese.

Suggested wine: Merlot

Recipe Notes

Recipe Notes

Veal Scaloppini with Vegetables

Serves 4

VEAL

8 thinly sliced veal scallopines or veal pounded thin

$^1/_2$ cup flour

2 egg yolks

I tablespoon olive oil

Salt and pepper

$^2/_3$ cup milk

Dip veal into flour and shake off excess. Mix egg yolks, oil, milk and salt and pepper. Heat frying pan to 375°F. Add oil and some butter to pan to at least ¼ inches deep. Dip veal into batter and fry quickly for about 2 minutes on each side or until golden. Drain on crumpled paper towels.

VEGETABLES

$^1/_4$ cup butter

I pound sliced mushrooms

Salt and pepper

I lemon, peeled and cut into slices

2 heads fennel, cut into I-inch slices and blanched for 5 minutes

2 dozen frozen baby artichokes (if using fresh, blanch for 5 minutes)

$^1/_4$ cup dry Marsala

Parmesan cheese

Heat butter and sauté mushrooms. Sprinkle with salt and pepper and add lemon slices. When mushrooms have rendered their moisture, add Marsala, fennel, artichokes and bring back to high heat. Cook until fennel and artichokes are tender. Remove to plates and sprinkle with Parmesan cheese.

Veal Scaloppini with Vegetables — continued

GARNISH

Lemon slices

Chopped parsley

2 slices of prosciutto, julienne sliced

Plate veal along with the vegetables. Garnish with chopped parsley, lemon slices and prosciutto.

Osso Bucco (Veal Shanks)

Serves 6

6 veal shanks

Flour

Olive oil

¹/₂ cup butter

I carrot, finely chopped

2 small onions, finely chopped

I large garlic clove, smashed

¹/₂ cup dry white wine

I cup tomatoes, peeled and seeded or I large can pear shaped tomatoes

I teaspoon orange rind

I teaspoon saffron threads

¹/₂ teaspoon dried basil

I tablespoon parsley with stems, chopped

Chicken or veal stock

Flour veal on both sides. Heat olive oil in large skillet and brown veal shanks on both sides until golden. Discard oil and replace it with the butter. Cook the diced carrots, onion until light golden. Add garlic and veal shanks. Add wine and increase heat to high heat until only few tablespoons of wine remain. Add tomatoes, orange rind, saffron with 1 cup stock. If stock does not reach half way up pieces of meat, add more stock until you reach this mark. Add dried basil and parsley stems. Add salt and pepper to taste.

Cover with foil and pot lid and bake in 325°F oven for about 1½ to 2 hours.

Sprinkle with Gremolada, if desired, and heat through. Serve with risotto or rice.

Gremolada

I clove garlic, finely chopped

I tablespoon parsley, chopped

Rind of ½ lemon, finely grated

2 small anchovy filets, rinsed (or use I teaspoon anchovy paste)

Mix together and top veal shanks.

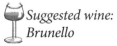
Suggested wine: Brunello

Recipe Notes

Moussaka

Serves 8

3 medium eggplants, sliced

1 cup butter, divided

3 large onions, finely chopped

2 pounds ground lamb or beef

3 tablespoons tomato paste

½ cup red wine

½ cup parsley, chopped

¼ teaspoon cinnamon

6 tablespoons flour

1 quart milk

4 eggs, beaten until frothy

Pinch of nutmeg

2 cups ricotta cheese

1 cup fine breadcrumbs

1 cup Parmesan cheese, grated

Peel eggplants and cut into slices about ½-inch thick. Melt 4 tablespoons of butter in skillet and brown eggplant slices quickly. Set aside.

Heat 4 tablespoons butter in skillet and cook onions until brown. Add meat and cook 10 minutes. Combine tomato paste, wine, parsley, cinnamon, salt and pepper. Stir mixture into meat and simmer on low heat until all liquid is absorbed. Remove mixture from heat.

Preheat oven to 375°F. Make white sauce by melting 8 tablespoons of butter and blending in flour, stirring with wire whisk. Slowly add milk, stirring constantly. When mixture has thickened and is smooth, remove from heat. Cool slightly, stir in beaten eggs, nutmeg and ricotta cheese.

Grease 11x6-inch pan and sprinkle bottom lightly with breadcrumbs. Arrange alternate layers of eggplant and meat sauce to pan, sprinkling each layer with Parmesan cheese and breadcrumbs. Pour ricotta cheese sauce over the top and bake 1 hour or until top is golden. Remove from oven and cool 20 minutes before serving.

This is a good choice for a party since it is an excellent make ahead dish! It is actually better the second day!

Suggested wine: Rosé or another light red wine

Balsamic Glazed Duck Breasts with Onion Pear Hash

Serves 4

4 duck breasts

2 tablespoons olive oil

2 ripe pears, halved, cored, cut into ¼-inch slices

I bag (IO-ounce) pearl onions, blanched, peeled, halved

4 medium Yukon Gold potatoes (about I½ pounds), boiled until just tender, peeled, cut into I¼-inch pieces

2 tablespoons fresh sage, chopped

¾ cup low-salt chicken broth

½ cup balsamic vinegar

Using small sharp knife, score duck skin in 1-inch-wide grid pattern. Season duck generously with salt and pepper. Heat oil in large skillet over medium-high heat. Add duck; cook about 6 minutes per side for medium. Transfer to cutting board; tent with foil. Discard all but ¼ cup drippings from skillet. Heat drippings in skillet over high heat. Add pears, onions, and potatoes; sauté until beginning to brown, 5 minutes. Stir in sage; season with salt and pepper. Transfer hash to bowl; cover to keep warm.

Heat same skillet over high heat. Add broth and vinegar; bring to boil, scraping up browned bits. Boil until reduced to glaze, about 5 minutes. Season glaze with salt and pepper.

Divide hash among plates. Cut duck into ½-inch-thick slices; fan over hash. Drizzle glaze over and serve.

Suggested wine: Pinot Noir

Recipe Notes

Duck with Port Cherry Sauce

Serves 4

I cup soy sauce

I cup sherry

4 (6-ounce) duck breast halves

12 frozen dark sweet cherries, thawed, halved

I cup chicken stock or canned low-salt chicken broth

I cup beef stock or canned beef broth

$^1/_2$ cup ruby port

I fresh thyme sprig

I teaspoon cornstarch dissolved in 2 teaspoons water

$^1/_4$ cup ($^1/_2$ stick) butter, cut into $^1/_2$-inch pieces, room temperature

Whisk soy sauce and sherry in medium bowl to blend. Using sharp knife, make diagonal cuts at 1/2-inch intervals in duck skin (not through meat). Place duck, skin side up, in glass baking dish. Pour marinade over. Cover duck with plastic wrap and refrigerate at least 2 hours and up to 6 hours.

Bring cherries, chicken stock, beef stock, port and thyme sprig to boil in heavy medium saucepan over high heat. Simmer until mixture is reduced to ½ cup, about 15 minutes.

Meanwhile, heat heavy large skillet over medium heat. Remove duck from marinade. Add duck breasts, skin side down, to skillet. Cook until skin is crispy, about 10 minutes. Turn duck over and continue cooking to desired doneness, about 5 minutes for medium. Transfer duck to work surface.

Add cornstarch mixture to port-cherry sauce. Bring to simmer, whisking constantly. Add butter 1 piece at a time, whisking until butter is melted before adding next piece. Season sauce to taste with salt and pepper.

Slice duck breasts thinly on diagonal and fan out on plates. Spoon port-cherry sauce over duck and serve.

Cooking an entire duck can be greasy. You can now find duck breasts in the meat section of most supermarkets or you can ask your butcher to remove the breasts from the duck. This is a delightful and less greasy way to cook duck!

Suggested wine: Pinot Noir

Gruyère Chicken Dish

Serves 12

6 whole boneless chicken breasts (12 halves), skinned

Flour and butter

8+ tablespoons unsalted butter, divided

4 large onions, chopped

2 cups Parmesan cheese, shredded

2 cups Gruyère cheese, shredded

2 teaspoons sweet Hungarian paprika

1 cup dried breadcrumbs

1 cup dry white wine

1½ cups chicken stock

Flour the chicken breasts. Melt butter in a large skillet and brown the chicken breasts. Set aside. In same skillet, melt 4 tablespoons butter and sauté the onions until golden.

Mix together the Parmesan cheese, Gruyère cheese, paprika and breadcrumbs.

Butter a large casserole dish; large enough for the chicken to lay in one layer. You may need two dishes. Preheat oven to 375°F.

Layer ½ of the onions into the bottom of the casserole. Place the chicken on top. Cover with remaining onions. Sprinkle cheese mixture on top. Dot with 4 tablespoons of butter.

Mix the wine and chicken stock together. Drizzle over the dish. Bake uncovered for 1 hour. Let rest in oven at 200 degrees for an additional 15 to 20 minutes.

This is wonderful served with parsley orzo and a green salad.

Recipe Notes

Recipe Notes

Grilled Chicken with Peach and Apple Salsa

Serves 4

CHICKEN

3 tablespoons olive oil

2 tablespoons dry white wine

2 tablespoons fresh lime juice

1 tablespoon Worcestershire sauce

1 1/2 teaspoons dried basil

4 boneless chicken breast halves

Mix first 5 ingredients in large bowl. Add chicken and turn to coat. Cover and chill at least 1 hour. (Can be prepared 4 hours ahead. Keep refrigerated.)

SALSA

2 large ripe peaches

1 small Granny Smith apple, peeled, cored, and chopped

1/2 cup fresh chopped cilantro

3 1/2 tablespoons honey

2 tablespoons fresh lime juice

1/4 teaspoon ground allspice

1/4 teaspoon ground cinnamon

Bring medium saucepan of water to boil. Add peaches; cook 30 seconds. Using slotted spoon, transfer peaches to bowl of cold water. Drain peaches. Peel and chop coarsely. Place peaches in large bowl. Mix in remaining salsa ingredients.

Prepare barbecue grill (medium high-heat). Remove chicken from marinade. Grill chicken until just cooked through, about 5 minutes per side. Transfer to plates. Serve with salsa.

 Suggested wine: Italian white

Chicken Touraine

Serves 6 to 8

2 pounds chicken pieces

2 tablespoons butter

I teaspoon vegetable oil

I medium onion, chopped

I 1/2 cups mushrooms, sliced

I teaspoon salt

1/4 teaspoon black pepper

I teaspoon paprika

1/2 cup white wine

1/2 cup sour cream

I can (32 ounces) diced tomatoes

I teaspoon flour

Brown chicken in butter and oil. Remove and keep warm. Brown onion, add tomatoes, wine, salt, pepper and paprika. Simmer 15 minutes. Add chicken and simmer additional 20 minutes. Add mushrooms and cook 10 minutes. Combine sour cream and flour and stir into the stew. Heat thoroughly.

Serve with crispy French bread and simple salad.

Suggested wine: white Burgundy

Recipe Notes

Recipe Notes

Chicken Stir-Fry

Serves 4

¹/₄ cup orange juice

1¹/₂ tablespoons cornstarch

1 pound skinless, boneless chicken breasts, cut into strips

³/₄ cup reduced-sodium chicken broth

1¹/₂ tablespoons reduced-sodium soy sauce

2¹/₂ teaspoons vegetable oil

1 clove garlic, minced

1 tablespoon fresh ginger, peeled and minced or 1¹/₂ teaspoons ground ginger

1¹/₂ cups snow peas or green beans

1 medium red bell pepper, cut into thin strips

1 cup carrots, sliced

³/₄ cup green onion, sliced

2 cups cooked white rice

In a shallow glass bowl, combine the orange juice and cornstarch; mix well. Stir in chicken. Cover bowl with plastic wrap and refrigerate for 2 hours.

Drain chicken; discard juice mixture. In a small bowl, combine broth and soy sauce. Set aside.

In a wok or large nonstick skillet, heat oil over medium heat. Add garlic and ginger; stir-fry for 30 seconds. Add chicken; stir-fry for 3 minutes. Add vegetables; stir-fry until crisp-tender, about 5 minutes. Stir in broth mixture.

Serve chicken mixture over rice in individual bowls.

Country French Chicken

Serves 4

2 tablespoons butter	I tablespoon parsley, finely chopped
3 pounds frying chicken, cut into quarters	I bay leaf
16 small white onions	I teaspoon salt
4 small carrots, peeled and cut diagonally into I¹/₂-inch pieces	¹/₄ teaspoon pepper
2 cloves garlic, minced	¹/₄ teaspoon dried thyme leaves, crushed
2 tablespoons brandy	¹/₈ teaspoon ground cloves
2 cups dry white wine	8 ounces sugar snap peas

In large skillet over medium high heat, melt butter. Add chicken pieces, skin side down, and brown, turning chicken to brown all sides. Transfer browned chicken to baking dish. Set aside. In skillet with pan drippings, sauté carrots, onions and garlic until lightly browned.

Add brandy to skillet. If you feel comfortable and are adventurous, flame brandy by carefully tipping pan to ignite with gas burner or by quickly placing lighter near liquid. Otherwise, raise heat for approximately 1 minute and then reduce heat. Add wine, parsley, bay leaf, salt and pepper, thyme and cloves.

Increase heat to high and bring carrot mixture to boil, stirring frequently. Remove skillet from heat and with large spoon, transfer carrot mixture to chicken in baking dish.

Preheat oven to 350°F. Cover baking dish with foil and bake for 30 minutes. Uncover dish and distribute peas over chicken. Cover again and continue to bake an additional 30 minutes. Remove bay leaf. Serve and enjoy.

Suggested wine: red Burgundy

Recipe Notes

Recipe Notes

Chicken Breasts Stuffed with Perfection

Serves 6

6 skinless, boneless chicken breast halves — pounded thin

I bottle (**8** ounce) Italian-style salad dressing

8 slices of stale wheat bread, torn

3/4 cup Parmesan cheese, grated

I teaspoon fresh thyme, chopped

1/8 teaspoon pepper

1 1/2 cups feta cheese, crumbled

1/2 cup sour cream

I tablespoon vegetable oil

3 cloves garlic, minced

4 cups fresh spinach, chopped

I bunch green onions, chopped

I cup mushrooms, sliced

I jar (**8** ounce) oil-packed sun-dried tomatoes, chopped

Place chicken breasts in a large re-sealable plastic bag. Pour in Italian dressing, seal tightly, and refrigerate at least 1 hour. Place the stale bread, Parmesan, thyme, and pepper into a food processor. Pulse until the bread is processed into crumbs. (You may use purchased breadcrumbs.) Set aside. In a large bowl, stir together the feta and sour cream. Set aside. Heat the oil in a large skillet over medium heat. Stir in the garlic. Then add the spinach, and cook until it wilts. Stir in green onions, cook 2 minutes. Remove spinach to a plate, and leave any liquid in the pan. Stir in mushrooms, and sauté until soft. Remove mushrooms to plate with spinach. Allow to cool briefly, then combine spinach and mushrooms with feta and sour cream mixture. Stir the sun-dried tomatoes into the mixture, and spread onto a large cookie sheet. Place in the freezer for about 30 minutes.

Preheat the oven to 400° F. Place chicken breasts on a cookie sheet, and place about 3 tablespoons of the filling mixture in the center of each breast. Roll the breasts, and secure with a toothpick. Transfer chicken breasts to a baking dish, and sprinkle breadcrumb mixture over chicken breasts. Bake uncovered, for 25 minutes.

Chicken Breast Cutlets with Artichokes and Capers

Serves 6

I cup whole wheat or white flour

$^1/_2$ teaspoon salt

$^1/_8$ teaspoon white pepper, or to taste

$^1/_8$ teaspoon black pepper, or to taste

2 pounds chicken breast tenderloins or strips

2 tablespoons canola oil

2 tablespoons extra-virgin olive oil

2 cups chicken broth

2 tablespoons fresh lemon juice

I jar (12 ounce) quartered marinated artichoke hearts, with liquid

$^1/_4$ cup capers

2 tablespoons butter

$^1/_4$ cup flat-leaf parsley, chopped

Combine flour, salt, and white and black peppers. Dredge chicken in seasoned flour and shake off excess. Heat canola oil and olive oil in a large skillet over medium-high heat. Add chicken breasts and cook until golden brown on both sides, and no longer pink on the inside; set aside. Pour in chicken broth and lemon juice. Bring to a simmer, scraping the bottom of the pan to dissolve the caramelized bits. Add artichoke hearts and capers, return to a simmer, and cook until reduced by half. Whisk butter into sauce until melted. Place cooked chicken back into pan, and simmer in the sauce for a few minutes to reheat. Serve on a platter sprinkled with chopped fresh parsley.

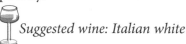 *Suggested wine: Italian white*

Recipe Notes

Chicken Tortilla Casserole

Serves 8 to 10

2 medium onions, chopped

1/2 cup chopped celery

1 cup reduced sodium chicken broth

6 boneless skinless chicken breast halves

10 (6 inch) corn tortillas, torn into bite size pieces

2 cans (4 ounces) diced green chile peppers, drained

1 can reduced sodium condensed cream of chicken soup

2 cups shredded cheese (Mexican Mix or jack and Cheddar is fine), divided

1 teaspoon pepper

1 cup salsa (chipotle salsa adds a nice flavor)

1 can sliced olives (optional)

1 teaspoon pepper

Poach the chicken breasts in water until cooked thoroughly. Wait until cool, cut into bite-size pieces. Meanwhile, in a medium saucepan combine onions, celery and chicken broth. Simmer covered 5 to 6 minutes until veggies are tender.

In a large bowl, stir together undrained onion mixture, chicken, tortillas, chile peppers, olives, cream of chicken soup, one cup of cheese and pepper. Transfer mixture to a lightly greased 9x13-inch baking pan. Top with salsa and remaining cheese.

Bake in 350°F oven approximately 30 minutes. Let stand 5 minutes before slicing.

Great to make ahead and reheat — tastes even better the second day! I serve with a simple Caesar salad. This recipe feeds a crowd.

Chicken Pot Pie

Serves 8

3 pounds cooked chicken, cubed

4 tablespoons unsalted butter, divided

I cup carrots, diced

I cup celery, sliced

I cup onion, diced

I cup mushrooms, sliced

Salt and pepper to taste

6 tablespoons flour

$^1/_2$ cup dry white wine

3 cups chicken stock

I cup light cream

I sheet puff pastry, thawed

In large saucepan, melt half of the butter and sauté the carrots, celery and onion until they begin to soften. Add the mushrooms and continue to cook for 4 minutes. Season with salt and pepper.

Add the remaining butter, stir until melted and sprinkle the flour over the vegetables. Cook, stirring for approximately 2 minutes. Add the wine. Stir to incorporate the flour, add the chicken stock and stir to combine. Reduce the heat and simmer until the vegetables become tender and the sauce thickens, about 15 minutes. Add the light cream and bring to a boil. Add the chicken, cook until heated through. Season to taste with salt and pepper. Place the chicken mixture into individual ramekins (the size you deem best for an individual portion).

Preheat the oven to 400°F. Roll out the puff pastry until ⅛-inch thick. Cut into 8 individual circles. Bake the puff pastry for 20 minutes.

Place one puff pastry onto the chicken mixture in their individual ramekins.

Suggested wine: Sauvignon Blanc

You may also place the mixture into a 9x13-inch baking dish. Roll the puff pastry out to slightly fit the 9x13-inch dish. Carefully, place the puff pastry onto a cookie sheet and bake for 20 minutes. Remove carefully and place over the chicken mixture.

Moroccan Chicken with Couscous and Vegetables

Serves 6

I whole chicken, cut into pieces

4 cups chicken broth

3$^{1}/_{2}$ tablespoons butter, divided

$^{1}/_{4}$ cup vegetable oil

I large onion, cut into wedges

$^{1}/_{2}$ pound plum tomatoes, quartered

I cup parsley, finely chopped

I$^{1}/_{2}$ teaspoons ground ginger

I$^{1}/_{2}$ teaspoons black pepper

I teaspoon turmeric

I jalapeño chile pepper

$^{1}/_{2}$ cinnamon stick

$^{1}/_{4}$ teaspoon cayenne pepper

$^{1}/_{2}$ cup golden raisins

$^{1}/_{8}$ teaspoon saffron threads, crushed

5 turnips, peeled and quartered

4 large carrots, peeled, quartered and cut crosswise

I acorn squash, peeled, seeded and cut into 2-inch pieces

3 zucchini, chopped into medium pieces

I can (16 ounce) garbanzo beans

2$^{1}/_{4}$ cups water

I$^{1}/_{2}$ teaspoons salt

3 cups couscous

Combine chicken and broth in large Dutch oven. Simmer chicken, turning occasionally, about 20 minutes. Remove chicken from cooking liquid; reserve cooking liquid. Skin and bone chicken. Cut into bite size pieces. (Can be prepared 1 day ahead. Store broth and chicken separately.)

Melt 2 tablespoons butter with oil in Dutch oven over medium high heat. Add onion and sauté until tender. Add tomatoes, parsley, ginger, pepper, turmeric, chile pepper, cinnamon stick and cayenne pepper and stir for 1 minute. Mix in reserved chicken broth, turnips, squash, zucchini, carrots, garbanzo beans and raisins. Cover and simmer until vegetables are tender, about 15 minutes. Uncover and continue to cook for 5 additional minutes. Add chicken pieces to sauce and cook until heated through. Discard jalapeño pepper.

Moroccan Chicken with Couscous and Vegetables — continued

Meanwhile, bring water, 1½ tablespoons butter and salt to boil in medium saucepan. Stir in couscous. Remove from heat, cover and let stand for 10 minutes. Fluff with fork.

Arrange couscous on center of serving platter. Spoon chicken and vegetables over couscous. If you feel there is too much liquid, remove some of the sauce and pass separately. Perfect for a dinner party; serve with Merlot!

Chicken on Linguine with Walnut Sauce

Serves 4

2 tablespoons olive oil

I package boneless, skinless chicken tenders

I red bell pepper, diced

2 shallots, chopped

¼ teaspoon ground nutmeg

¼ teaspoon cayenne pepper

½ cup walnuts, chopped, divided

½ cup fresh or frozen peas

²/₃ cup whipping cream

½ cup chicken broth

½ pound linguine or angel hair pasta

½ cup Parmesan cheese, grated

In a large skillet, heat oil over high heat. Sauté chicken until cooked through which takes about 5 minutes. Transfer chicken to a plate. Cook bell pepper, shallots, nutmeg and cayenne in skillet for about 5 minutes or until the pepper begins to soften. Add ¼ cup of the walnuts and the peas. Add the broth and cream and cook until it thickens into a sauce consistency (about 5 minutes).

At the same time, cook the linguine or angel hair. Mix the pasta, remaining walnuts, the chicken and the sauce. Sprinkle with cheese and serve.

Suggested wine: Italian white

Fran's French Lasagna

Serves 8 to 12 hungry skiers!

A nice alternative to traditional lasagna. A variation is to add thinly sliced prosciutto to each layer on top of the chicken. Can be made ahead; reheats well.

6 boneless, skinless chicken breast halves

2 packages frozen chopped spinach

¹/₂ pound mushrooms, sliced

2 onions, chopped

2 cups ricotta cheese

¹/₂ pound mozzarella cheese (hard, not soft or buy pre-grated)

¹/₂ pound Parmesan cheese (wedge or buy pre-grated)

2 cans cream of mushroom soup

2 cups sour cream

I package lasagna noodles

I tablespoon minced garlic

¹/₂ stick butter

I bottle inexpensive white wine

2 eggs

Poach chicken in white wine 45 to 60 minutes. Cool and tear into bite-size pieces. Cook spinach and drain well. Sauté onions, mushrooms and garlic in butter. Combine spinach with mushroom mixture. Grate mozzarella and Parmesan together. Blend ricotta with eggs. Blend soup and sour cream together over low heat. Cook lasagna noodles and drain.

Layer in large rectangular baking pan in the following order (do twice): soup mixture, noodles, chicken, spinach mixture, ricotta mixture and grated cheeses. Bake at 350°F approximately 1 hour, first half covered, second half uncovered.

Braised Pork in Apple Cider

Serves 6

3 pounds loin of pork

I teaspoon garlic powder

$^1/_2$ teaspoon paprika

I cup onions, quartered

I cup mushrooms, coarsely chopped

I cup carrots, cut Into rounds

I bay leaf

$^1/_2$ teaspoon rosemary

Salt and pepper to taste

I teaspoon dried thyme

I quart apple cider

3 sprigs of fresh parsley

$^1/_4$ cup flour

I beef bouillon cube

$^1/_4$ teaspoon nutmeg

I tablespoon butter

Rub pork with garlic powder and paprika and place in a deep oven proof pan or Dutch oven. Add the onions, carrots, bay leaf, rosemary, salt, pepper, thyme, apple cider and parsley. Cover and let stand in refrigerator for 24 hours, turning meat occasionally.

Preheat oven to 400°F. Remove meat from marinade. Strain the liquid and reserve both the broth and vegetables. On stovetop, heat the Dutch oven and place the pork loin fat side down in it. Brown meat, turning once. Place pork, fat side down, in pan uncovered and bake for 30 minutes. Remove pork and pour off the fat. Add the chopped mushrooms to vegetables and add to casserole and return all to the oven and bake for 10 minutes uncovered. Sprinkle the vegetables with the flour and bake for 5 minutes longer. Add the beef bouillon cube to the cider marinade and stir into the vegetables and return the pork to the pan. Cover and bake 1 hour. Remove the meat and keep covered. Strain the sauce and reserve the vegetables. Pour the sauce into a saucepan and reduce over moderate heat for about 20 minutes. Add the nutmeg and butter. Slice the meat and serve with the sauce and vegetables.

Recipe Notes

Pork with Cranberry and Onion Sauce

Serves 6 to 8

Recipe Notes

4 - 5 pounds center cut pork loin

1 tablespoon butter

2 onions, sliced

1 can whole cranberry sauce

¹/₄ cup balsamic vinegar

1 cup vegetable broth (water or white wine can be used also)

2 sticks fresh rosemary

In a saucepan, sauté onions in butter until translucent, about 5 minutes. Add the balsamic vinegar, then the cranberry sauce, the broth and the rosemary. Simmer until it thickens into a sauce consistency. This will take about an hour. Before serving, remove the branch of the rosemary, trying to leave as much of the "leaf" as possible. Roast pork at 375°F for 1 hour and 45 minutes or until internal temperature reaches 150°. Slice the pork and serve the sauce as gravy on the side.

This looks beautiful with some fresh rosemary as garnish and a small amount of sauce drizzled over the roast.

Suggested wine: Pinot Noir

Hoisin Pork Roast with Green Scallions

Recipe Notes

Serves 4 to 6

I tablespoon olive oil

I (5½-pound) boneless pork shoulder (about 6½ pounds with bone), trimmed, tied to hold shape

¾ cup hoisin sauce

3 bunches scallions, cut on diagonal into 1-inch pieces

I teaspoon whole black peppercorns

¼ cup Scotch whisky

¾ cup (or more) water
Sliced scallions for garnish

Preheat oven to 300°F. Heat oil in heavy large ovenproof pot over high heat. Add pork shoulder, fat side down; brown on all sides, turning often, about 12 minutes. Remove pot from heat. Spread hoisin sauce over pork; sprinkle with scallion pieces and peppercorns. Add ½ cup water, cover pot and place in oven. Cook until pork is very tender when pierced with fork, about 2¾ hours, adding water to pot by ¼ cupfuls if mixture is dry. Remove pot from oven. Transfer pork to cutting board and tent with foil. Let pork stand 20 minutes. Meanwhile, spoon off fat from pan juices. Stir whisky and ¾ cup water into juices; boil 2 minutes. Add more water by tablespoonfuls if sauce is too thick, or boil to reduce sauce if too thin. Cut pork crosswise on slight diagonal into 1-inch-thick slices. Garnish with sliced green onions. Pour pan sauce over pork and serve.

Spicy Asian Marinated Pork Loins

Serves 6 to 8

Recipe Notes

2 pork tenderloins

MARINADE
$^{1}/_{2}$ **cup soy sauce**

2 tablespoons sugar

$^{1}/_{2}$ **large onion, minced**

2 teaspoons oriental chili paste with garlic

I tablespoon oriental sesame oil

SAUCE
3 tablespoons soy sauce

2 tablespoons rice (wine) vinegar

I tablespoon oriental sesame oil

I tablespoon oriental chili paste with garlic

I tablespoon fresh ginger, grated

4 scallions, sliced finely

Marinate the pork tenderloins for 3 hours. Grill over hot coals, using judgment about firmness and when to turn and apply remaining marinade (approximately 10 minutes on each side).

Serve with sauce and steamed rice.

Get an Asian automatic rice pot, it cooks in 20 minutes and keeps rice warm!

Suggested wine: Zinfandel

Renee's Company Pork Tenderloin

Serves 4 to 6

I large or 2 small pork tenderloin

16 bay leaves

2 tablespoons olive oil

I bottle red wine, Cabernet, Merlot or Zinfandel

Salt and pepper

Kitchen twine

This recipe gets its name because it is a crowd pleaser yet very easy to make if you are entertaining on a busy weeknight. Doubles easily.

Preheat oven to 400°F. Rub tenderloin with olive oil, sprinkle with salt and pepper. Place in roasting pan. Place bay leaves over pork and secure with kitchen twine by crisscrossing from end to end. Pour in bottle of red wine.

Cook for 50 to 60 minutes or until pork is done to your liking. Remove string and bay leaves. Slice pork into thin slices and arrange on plates.

Serve with roasted potatoes, page 83.

Suggested wine: Pinot Noir

Recipe Notes

Stuffed Baked Ham

Serves a Crowd

I fully cooked IO pound ham

IO ounces frozen chopped kale or fresh kale, chopped and steamed

I cup spinach, finely chopped

I large onion, finely chopped

³/₄ cup watercress, finely chopped

¹/₂ cup celery tops, finely chopped

¹/₂ teaspoon salt

¹/₄ teaspoon pepper

Trim rind/fat from ham. Make x-shaped cuts 2 inches deep all over sides, top and bottom.

Cook kale in salted, boiling water; drain, cool and squeeze water out. Combine kale, spinach, onion, watercress, celery, salt and pepper. Take small amounts of mixture and press into the x-cuts all over the ham.

GLAZE

¹/₂ cup honey

2 tablespoons vinegar

2 teaspoons dry mustard

Bake ham 2 hours at 325°F, brushing with the glaze during last 30 minutes. Remove from oven, and let rest for 30 minutes. Carve carefully.

You may use a spiral ham, just place the kale mixture between the layers. Only bake for 1 hour and glaze after 30 minutes.

If you have additional kale mixture left over, place in bottom of pan and place ham over the kale. Makes a delicious side dish or extra vegetable for the ham.

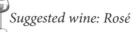 *Suggested wine: Rosé*

Choucroute Garnie
(Sauerkraut with Pork and Sausage)

Serves 6

2 pounds Morse's sauerkraut (see note, or use sauerkraut sold in plastic bags or in jars)

¹/₂ pound bacon, coarsely chopped

I large onion, chopped

4 carrots, peeled and sliced

I Granny Smith apple, skin on and grated

2 tablespoons gin

4 parsley springs

8 peppercorns

2 bay leaves

I cup dry white wine

4 cups chicken stock (may need more during cooking process)

2 pounds bratwurst or knackwurst or other sausage

6 boneless pork chops

Soak the sauerkraut in cold water for approximately 30 minutes. Fry the bacon in a large skillet for about 5 minutes. Add the onions and carrots until lightly browned. Drain the sauerkraut and thoroughly squeeze out the water. Spread kraut in non-aluminum roaster or Dutch oven with tight fitting lid. Add bacon, bacon fat, vegetables, apples, gin, parsley, peppercorns and bay leaves. Pour in wine and enough chicken stock to cover the kraut.

Preheat oven to 325°F. Place buttered wax paper over kraut. Do not use foil. Cover with lid and cook for 5 hours, adding more stock if dish appears to be drying out. All liquid should be absorbed by end of cooking time.

With approximately 45 minutes to end of cooking time, prick sausage skins and add to pot along with the pork chops. When done, remove from oven, remove bay leaves, parsley sprigs and sprinkle with the chopped parsley.

Serve with mashed potatoes.

Suggested wine: Riesling (Alsatian)

Morse's Sauerkraut is made in Waldoboro, Maine. In the fall, you can stop by and see the various stages of sauerkraut production. The sauerkraut can be ordered by calling 207-832-5569 and can also be found in local grocery stores. It is the best!

Recipe Notes

Fish Pot Pie

Serves 6 to 8

2 tablespoons butter

I large fennel bulb, trimmed, halved, thinly sliced crosswise

¹/₂ cup sliced shallots (2 medium)

2 tablespoons flour

I cup vegetable broth

I¹/₂ pounds halibut fillets cut into I-inch cubes

I package (6 ounce) fresh baby spinach

3¹/₂ cups mashed potatoes

Preheat broiler. Melt butter in a large, deep, heavy saucepan over medium heat. Add fennel and shallots; cover and cook until tender, about 8 minutes, stirring occasionally. Sprinkle in flour, salt and pepper and sauté 2 minutes. Add broth, bring to a boil stirring often, and add fish and spinach. Cover and simmer over medium heat until the fish is almost cooked through (about 4 minutes). Transfer fish mixture to an 11x7x2-inch baking dish. Spoon mashed potatoes over the top. Broil until filling bubbles at the edges and the potatoes are browned in spots (about 4 minutes).

Suggested wine: Sauvignon Blanc

Thai Halibut with Coconut-Curry Sauce

Serves 4

2 teaspoons olive oil	4 halibut steaks
³/₄ cup shallots, finely chopped	¹/₂ cup cilantro, chopped
1¹/₂ teaspoons red curry paste (or to taste)	2 scallions, sliced
2 cups chicken broth	2 tablespoons lime juice
¹/₂ cup light coconut milk	Black pepper
¹/₂ teaspoon salt	2 cups cooked jasmine rice
	6 cups baby spinach, steamed

In large sauté pan, heat oil over moderate heat and cook shallots until beginning to brown. Add the curry paste and stir for about 30 seconds. Add the chicken broth, coconut milk, salt and simmer until sauce is reduced to 2 cups.

Add the halibut to the sauce and gently cook; carefully turning the fish over to coat both sides. Cook until the halibut flakes easily, approximately 9 minutes. Remove the fish to a platter and cover with foil. Add the cilantro, scallions and lime juice to the sauce and season with salt and pepper.

To plate: using large shallow bowls, place the rice in the bottom of the bowl. Top with spinach and then the fish. Spoon the sauce over the fish.

Suggested wine: Gewürztraminer

Recipe Notes

Chili-Roasted Cod

Serves 4

2 pounds fresh cod fillets (about ³/₄-inch thick)

I tablespoon chili powder

¹/₂ teaspoon dried oregano

¹/₂ teaspoon salt

2 tablespoons butter

¹/₄ teaspoon cumin

Juice of I lime

Heat oven to 450°F. Lightly coat a roasting pan with spray olive oil. Arrange fillets skin side down. Sprinkle with chili powder so most of fish is covered. Sprinkle with salt and oregano. Roast 5 to 7 minutes or until cod is just opaque and flakes when tested with a fork.

Meanwhile, melt the butter in a small saucepan over medium-low heat. Add cumin and lime juice and cook 1 minute longer. Remove cod from oven and drizzle the cumin-lime butter over it. Serve immediately.

Suggested wine: Sauvignon Blanc

This is a very easy dish that is fast to make and delicious. I often make it for company after a busy work day. You may substitute any chunky white fish, such as haddock.

Grilled Marinated Bluefish

Serves 4

2 pounds bluefish fillet

¹/₄ cup orange juice

¹/₄ cup soy sauce

2 tablespoons ketchup

2 tablespoons oil

2 tablespoons parsley

2 tablespoons lime juice

I clove garlic, crushed

¹/₂ teaspoon oregano

¹/₂ teaspoon pepper

Combine all ingredients and marinate bluefish fillet for 30 minutes. Grill on tin foil over medium heat for 15 to 30 minutes.

A great way to grill fresh bluefish but excellent for chicken or pork as well!

Maple-Seasoned Salmon with Rosemary-Orange Glaze

Serves 2

$^{1}/_{2}$ - $^{3}/_{4}$ pound salmon fillet, skinned

2 tablespoons flour

Salt and pepper

1 tablespoon butter

$^{1}/_{2}$ cup orange juice, freshly squeezed

$^{1}/_{4}$ cup Chardonnay

$^{1}/_{2}$ teaspoon fresh rosemary, chopped

1 tablespoon shallots, minced

1 tablespoon maple syrup

In a shallow bowl, combine flour, salt, and pepper. Dredge salmon in flour mixture, brush off excess flour and set aside. In a skillet melt butter over medium heat. Add salmon and sauté for 1 to 2 minutes per side. Remove salmon from pan. Add orange juice, Chardonnay, rosemary and shallots to same pan, and boil until liquid is reduced by half, about 3 minutes. Stir in maple syrup. Cut salmon in half and serve topped with sauce.

Substitute 1 whole boneless chicken breast, pounded flat, for the salmon.

Suggested wine: Sauvignon Blanc

Horseradish Encrusted Salmon with Spinach Salad

Serves 6

SALMON

4 inches fresh horseradish root, peeled and grated

2 tablespoons olive oil

6 (8 ounce) salmon filets

Add the oil to the grated horseradish and mix well. Pat the salmon dry and encrust the horseradish onto the flesh side. Chill for 1 hour.

SALAD

1 grapefruit

3 oranges

1 lemon

1 lime

½ cup canned Mandarin oranges

6 cups baby spinach

½ cup Japanese rice wine (Mirin)

1 shallot, minced

1 tablespoon fresh tarragon, chopped

Salt and pepper to taste

Peel and section the fruit and chop into small pieces. Add the Mandarin oranges. Save the juice from the canned oranges for the salad dressing. Combine the rice wine, shallot, tarragon and reserved juice. Whisk together and season with salt and pepper.

Heat skillet to medium, toss the fruit and dressing in the skillet and warm. Add the spinach to the skillet and let it wilt. Set aside. Meanwhile, heat olive oil in hot skillet. Place salmon filets, horseradish side down and sear for 3 minutes or until horseradish crust is golden brown. Reduce heat to medium, turn salmon over and cook for 5 to 7 minutes, depending on how you like your fish cooked.

To plate, place salad mixture into center of plate and place fish on top.

Suggested wine: New Zealand Sauvignon Blanc

Salmon Cakes

Serves 4

1½ cups poached salmon, flaked

1 scallion, thinly sliced

2 tablespoons parsley, chopped

1 tablespoon Dijon mustard

3 tablespoons mayonnaise

1 egg, slightly beaten

2 cups Panko crumbs (Japanese breadcrumbs), divided

Salt and pepper to taste

3 tablespoons olive oil

In a large bowl, combine salmon, scallion and parsley. In another bowl, blend the mustard and mayonnaise and season with salt and pepper. Gently add the mayonnaise mixture to the salmon mixture and stir together. Add ½ cup of Panko breadcrumbs and egg to the salmon. Shape into 4-6 cakes, depending on the size desired and chill for 1 hour.

Gently coat the salmon cakes in the remaining Panko breadcrumbs. Heat the oil in a skillet and cook the cakes on each side until golden brown.

Serve with a mixed green salad, tossed with lemon vinaigrette.

Suggested wine: Sauvignon Blanc

You may also serve with a spicy mayonnaise:

1 cup low fat mayonnaise

3 tablespoons chile sauce

1 tablespoon lemon juice

1 tablespoon fresh dill, chopped

Stir all the ingredients together and chill.

Crab Cakes
with Key Lime Aïoli

Serves 4

This is a good "make ahead" dish. The aïoli should be made at least 2 hours and the longer it sits in the fridge the better. The crab cakes can also be made ahead. Line a sheet pan or cookie sheet with waxed or parchment paper, pat out the cakes and arrange, then cover with plastic wrap and refrigerate until time to fry. Frying time is just a few minutes. (Note: can be made into bite size cakes and served as a finger food appetizer.)

1½ cups mayonnaise, divided

¼ cup plus 3 tablespoons Key lime juice

2 teaspoons garlic, minced, divided

1 tablespoon anchovy paste

3 teaspoons dry mustard, divided

2 tablespoons fresh parsley, chopped

2 tablespoons fresh dill, chopped

1 tablespoon olive oil

½ cup red bell pepper, finely diced

1 small yellow onion, finely diced

1 egg, lightly beaten

1 tablespoon Jamaican jerk seasoning (more or less to taste)

1 pound lump crabmeat, cooked

1 cup plain breadcrumbs

Vegetable oil for frying

In a bowl, combine 1 cup mayonnaise, ¼ cup lime juice, 1 teaspoon garlic, anchovy paste and 2 teaspoons dry mustard; mix until smooth. Stir in parsley, dill, salt and pepper to taste, cover and refrigerate.

In a fry pan over medium heat, warm olive oil. Add bell pepper, onion and remaining garlic, sauté until tender, about 5 minutes. Transfer to bowl and stir in ½ cup mayonnaise, egg, 3 tablespoons lime juice, jerk seasoning and 1 teaspoon mustard. Mix in crab, salt and pepper to taste and breadcrumbs. Shape into 3-inch diameter cakes. Should be covered and refrigerated at least an hour before frying.

In a large fry pan, pour in vegetable oil to ¼-inch depth. Fry about 1 minute per side, or until golden brown. Transfer to paper towels to drain. Serve crab cakes with aïoli alongside. Garnish with fresh dill or parsley. Doubles easily.

Suggested wine: Sauvignon Blanc

Seafood Salad

Serves 4

2 cups white wine

I cup water

¹/₂ pound thin asparagus

I pound sea scallops

I pound medium shrimp

2 ripe tomatoes, chopped

¹/₂ cup chopped, fresh basil

³/₄ cup olive oil

¹/₂ cup red wine vinegar

¹/₂ teaspoon salt

Pepper

Parsley

Lettuce

Recipe Notes

In large skillet, bring water and wine to a boil. Cut asparagus into 1-inch pieces and poach 3 to 5 minutes. Remove and set aside. Add the scallops to the skillet and poach 10 minutes. Add the shrimp and poach 5 more minutes.

In bowl, combine tomatoes, basil, oil, vinegar, salt and pepper. Toss together.

Drain seafood and toss with the tomato mixture as well as the asparagus.

Refrigerate at least 1 hour. It is best made 1 day ahead.

Place lettuce leaves on plate, mound the seafood mixture on the lettuce and garnish with chopped parsley.

Suggested wine: Sauvignon Blanc

Scallops with Red Onions

Serves 8

2¹/₂ pounds scallops

MARINADE

I cup water	I¹/₂ teaspoons ground ginger
¹/₄ cup lemon juice	¹/₂ teaspoon salt
2 tablespoons brown sugar	¹/₄ teaspoon white pepper
I¹/₂ tablespoons Worcestershire sauce	

Mix together the marinade ingredients and add to the scallops. Toss to coat. Marinate in refrigerator for 30 minutes.

ONIONS

3 tablespoons olive oil	Salt and pepper to taste
IO cups red onions, sliced thin	³/₄ cups red wine vinegar
I¹/₂ tablespoons brown sugar	I¹/₄ cups red wine

Heat the olive oil in a saucepan and add the onions. Cook over medium heat until they soften, about 10 minutes. Add the brown sugar and stir to coat. Season with salt and pepper. Continue to cook, stirring frequently, until onions are golden or about 10 to 15 additional minutes. Add the vinegar and cook until evaporated, add the red wine and cook to evaporate. Continue to stir the onions so they do not stick or burn. When the red wine has evaporated, remove from heat and keep warm. (This can be made at least 1 day ahead.)

Scallops with Red Onions— continued

Drain the scallops and pat dry. Heat a frying pan until hot. Rub a thin layer of oil on the pan and add the scallops. Do not overcrowd the scallops; you may have to do this in batches. Sear the scallops on each side until cooked to your liking.

To serve, arrange the warm onions onto a plate and top with the scallops.

Suggested wine: Pinot Noir

Pan-Seared Scallops Françoise

Serves 4

I pound dry deep sea scallops

2 tablespoons butter or light olive oil

2 - 4 tablespoons fresh lemon juice

2 - 4 tablespoons capers, drained from juice

Lemon wedges

Chopped parsley

Heat heavy skillet and melt butter. When sizzling, add scallops slowly so as not to allow pan to cool. Sear until brown on one side and turn. It may be necessary to brown in two batches. Remove scallops to a warmed plate. Quickly add lemon juice to pan to loosen any browned juices. Add capers. Stir. Pour over scallops. Serve with lemon wedges. Garnish with chopped parsley.

Suggested wine: Muscadet

Recipe Notes

Recipe Notes

Lobster with Pasta and Tarragon

Serves 6

2 tablespoons olive oil

$1/2$ cup chopped onion

I can (35 ounce) Italian plum tomatoes

2 teaspoons dried tarragon

Salt and pepper to taste

I cup heavy cream

2 tablespoons salt

I pound pasta

Pinch of cayenne pepper

$2^1/2$ cups chopped lobster meat

Heat the oil in a saucepan. Add the onions, reduce the heat, cover and cook until very tender. Chop and drain the tomatoes and add to the onions. Add the tarragon, season with salt and pepper and bring to a boil. Reduce the heat, cover and simmer, stirring occasionally for about 30 minutes. Remove the mixture from the heat and let cool. Puree the mixture in a food processor.

Return the purée to a saucepan, stir in the heavy cream. Simmer over medium heat, stirring often, for about 15 minutes or until slightly reduced. Correct the seasoning. Stir in the cayenne pepper and lobster. Simmer until lobster is heated.

Meanwhile, boil the pasta and drain. Spoon the sauce over the pasta.

Suggested wine: Chardonnay

Lobster Thermidor

Serves 4

5 pounds lobsters
(or I pound cooked lobster meat)

4 lemons

$^1/_2$ cup butter

$^1/_2$ cup flour

4 tablespoons minced shallots

$^1/_2$ cup white wine

4 cups whole milk

2 tablespoons Dijon mustard

2 tablespoons chopped fresh tarragon

I cup grated Parmesan cheese

Preheat the oven to 375°F. Butter 4 large ramekins or a small gratin dish. Bring a pot of salted water and lemon slices to a boil and add the lobsters. Cook for 8 to 12 minutes. Remove the lobsters and cool. Remove the lobster meat from the shells and chop.

In a saucepan, melt the butter. Stir in the flour and cook for 2 to 3 minutes to make a roux. Add the shallots and cook for 30 seconds. Slowly stir in the wine and milk. Bring the mixture to a boil and reduce to a simmer. Continue to cook until the sauce thickens; season with salt and pepper. Remove the sauce from the heat and stir in the mustard and tarragon. Add the chopped lobster meat. Stir in Parmesan cheese.

Divide the mixture between the 4 large ramekins or place into the gratin dish. Sprinkle with some additional cheese (about 1 tablespoon). Bake for 10 minutes or until the top is golden brown.

Suggested wine: Chardonnay (oaky)

Recipe Notes

Evalin's Traditional Lobster Rolls

Serves 4

If you can boil a pot of water, you can cook a Maine lobster!

The ratio of lobsters to the pot is important; a 4-5 gallon pot is ideal for steaming 6-8 pounds of lobster. Put 2 inches of seawater or salted water in the bottom of a large kettle and bring to a rolling boil over high heat. Put in the live lobsters, one at a time, cover the pot, and start timing. You definitely want to avoid overcooking or undercooking so to test for doneness, simply pull off one of the small legs; if it comes off easily, the lobster is ready. Drain the lobster and let cool.

Cooking times — (based on the 4-5 gallon pot)

1 pound — 10 minutes

1¼ pounds — 12 minutes

1½ pounds — 14 minutes

1¾ pounds — 16 minutes

2 pounds — 18 minutes

2½ pounds — 22 minutes

3 pounds — 25-30 minutes

5 pounds — 40-45 minutes

I pound picked lobster meat, cut into bite size chunks

I tablespoon freshly squeezed lemon juice

2 tablespoons mayonnaise

Salt and pepper to taste

4 top-split white hot dog buns

2 tablespoons unsalted butter

Mix lobster with lemon juice, mayonnaise and salt and pepper. Go sparingly with the mayonnaise, adding just enough to barely bind. Melt butter in small saucepan and brush on sides of rolls. Brown rolls on their sides in sauté pan over medium-high heat, until rolls are golden brown. Remove from pan with tongs and fill with lobster salad until rolls are bulging.

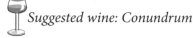 *Suggested wine: Conundrum*

Lobster Lasagna

Serves 8

2 pounds asparagus, trimmed

3 tablespoons olive oil

9 no-boil lasagna noodles

4 tablespoons butter

4 tablespoons flour

2 cups chicken stock

12 ounces Brie cheese, white skin removed, and chopped

1/4 cup sherry

12 ounces lobster meat

1 pound plum tomatoes, chopped

1 1/2 cups Parmesan cheese, grated

Preheat oven to 450°F. In baking pan, toss asparagus with olive oil and roast for 5 to 10 minutes, until crisp and tender. Sprinkle with salt and pepper and let cool. Cut into 2-inch pieces.

Reduce oven to 400°F.

In large bowl of warm water, let lasagna noodles soak for 10 minutes to soften. Drain.

In saucepan, melt butter and add the flour. Cook over low heat, stirring for 3 minutes to make a roux and cook the flour. Slowly add the chicken stock and whisk until sauce thickens. Add 1/3 of the Brie and whisk until melted and smooth. Repeat this process until all the cheese has been added. Add the sherry. Set aside.

Place noodles into bottom of 9x13-inch baking pan. Spread a thin layer of sauce (about 1/2 cup) over the noodles. Top with 1/2 of the asparagus, tomatoes and lobster. Sprinkle with Parmesan cheese. Place another layer of noodles, layer of sauce, asparagus, tomatoes and lobster. Sprinkle with Parmesan cheese. Top with additional noodles, remaining sauce and cheese.

Bake for 30 minutes or until golden brown and bubbling. Remove from oven and let stand 10 minutes before cutting and serving.

Suggested wine: Chardonnay (buttery)

Recipe Notes

Lobster Casserole

Serves 8 to 10

Recipe Notes

6 tablespoons unsalted butter, divided

4 tablespoons all-purpose flour

2 cups light cream

4 tablespoons Madeira or medium-dry sherry

I egg yolk

I tablespoon shallots, minced

I tablespoon parsley, minced

I teaspoon salt

$1/2$ teaspoon freshly ground black pepper

$1/2$ teaspoon celery seed

Dash of cayenne pepper

5 - 6 cups cooked lobster meat, cut into bite-size chunks

$1^{1}/_{2}$ cups fresh breadcrumbs

3 tablespoons Parmesan cheese, grated

Preheat oven to 400°F. Butter a shallow 2-quart baking dish. In a large saucepan or deep skillet, melt 4 tablespoons of the butter. Add the flour and cook over medium heat, whisking, for 2 minutes. Whisk in the cream, bring to a simmer, and cook, whisking, until the sauce is smooth and thick, 3 to 4 minutes. In a small bowl, whisk together the sherry and egg yolk. Whisk a little of the hot sauce in to temper the egg yolk, then whisk the egg yolk mixture into the hot sauce. Add the shallots, pepper, celery seed, and cayenne, and stir in the lobster meat. Transfer to the prepared baking dish, sprinkle with breadcrumbs and Parmesan cheese and drizzle with the remaining melted butter. (The casserole can be prepared up to 8 hours ahead to this point and refrigerated.) If cold, bake the casserole, loosely covered with foil for the first 15 minutes, until the sauce is bubbly and the crumbs are lightly browned, a total of about 35 minutes. If freshly prepared, bake uncovered for 20 to 25 minutes.

This makes a lovely presentation when baked in individual casserole dishes.

Suggested wine: Chardonnay

Vicky's Penne with Lobster in Cream Sauce

Serves 6

1 tablespoon olive oil

1 bunch scallions, chopped

8 ounces mushrooms, sliced

2 - 3 fresh tomatoes, seeded and chopped

1/2 bunch fresh basil, chopped (reserve a few whole leaves for garnish)

2 - 3 small zucchini, sliced (asparagus may be substituted)

1 box penne pasta (approximately 3/4 pound)

1 pound cooked lobster meat

1 pint heavy cream

8 ounces Parmesan cheese, grated

Shredded Parmesan cheese for garnish

4 ounces pre-made pesto

An easy way to treat out of town guests to the taste of lobster. Very rich and filling, serve with a simple green salad and fresh baguette.

Sauté scallions and mushrooms in olive oil. Mix with tomatoes, fresh basil and pesto; set aside. Steam zucchini to al dente, drain and add to above mixture.

Cook penne as directed on package. Drain penne. Add slightly heated or room temperature cream and cheese to penne.

While penne is cooking, cut lobster into bite size pieces, reserving whole claw pieces for garnish. Lightly sauté lobster in butter (do NOT overcook — it will toughen meat). Add reserved veggie mixture to lobster, then add both to penne, stir in well. Garnish with claw, small basil leaf and serve with shredded Parmesan cheese.

Suggested wine: Chardonnay (oaky)

Nutty Pasta with Shrimp

Serves 4

¾ cup fresh cilantro, minced

1½ tablespoons fresh ginger, peeled and grated

3 tablespoons low-sodium soy sauce

2 heaping tablespoons crunchy peanut butter

1 teaspoon sugar

1 teaspoon rice vinegar

1 teaspoon hot sauce

1 garlic clove, minced

2 teaspoons dark sesame oil

16 ounces large raw shrimp, peeled and de-veined

1 cup onion, sliced

1 red bell pepper, cut into (¼-inch) strips

1 bag baby spinach

10 ounces of angel hair pasta or rice noodles, cooked

Whisk first 8 ingredients in a medium bowl until well incorporated.

Heat oil in a large nonstick skillet over medium-high heat. Add shrimp and sauté for 3 minutes or until done and remove to plate. Add onion and bell pepper to pan and sauté for approximately 3 minutes. Add soy sauce mixture, shrimp and spinach. Reduce heat and cook until spinach is wilted. Toss with pasta and serve or divide pasta among 4 large bowls and divide shrimp mixture among the 4 bowls for individual servings.

Suggested wine: Gewürztraminer

Seafood Linguine

Serves 6 to 8

$^1/_2$ cup olive oil

$^1/_2$ cup unsalted butter

I large onion, chopped

6 garlic cloves, minced

I can (28 ounce) diced tomatoes

I cup dry white wine (may substitute with chicken broth)

$^1/_2$ cup fresh parsley, chopped (or about I tablespoon dried)

I - I$^1/_2$ pounds cooked or raw seafood (shrimp, scallops, lobster meat, etc.)

Dried rosemary and oregano to taste

Salt and pepper to taste

I pound linguine, cooked

Heat oil and butter in large pan. Add onions and sauté until tender. Add garlic and sauté for 1 minute. Add wine and cook until most of liquid has evaporated. Reduce heat, add tomatoes and spices. If using fresh parsley, add it just before serving. When mixture starts to simmer/bubble, add seafood and cook through. Serve immediately over cooked pasta.

Suggested wine: Chardonnay (oaky)

Recipe Notes

Crab and Herb Fettuccine

Serves 4

¹/₄ cup dry white wine

¹/₄ cup tarragon or white-wine vinegar

¹/₃ cup shallot, finely chopped

1¹/₄ sticks (10 tablespoons) cold unsalted butter, cut into tablespoon pieces

1 pound jumbo lump crabmeat, picked over

3 tablespoons fresh tarragon, chopped

3 tablespoons fresh chives, chopped

¹/₃ cup fresh flat-leaf parsley, chopped

1¹/₂ teaspoons fresh lemon zest, finely grated

3 tablespoons fresh lemon juice

¹/₂ teaspoon salt

¹/₂ pound egg fettuccine

Boil wine, vinegar, and shallot in a heavy saucepan over moderate heat until liquid is reduced to about 1 tablespoon, about 3 minutes. Add a few tablespoons butter, whisking constantly. Add remaining butter 1 piece at a time, whisking constantly and adding each new piece before previous one has completely melted, lifting pan from heat occasionally to cool mixture. Reduce heat to low, add crabmeat and cook, stirring occasionally, until just heated through, about 2 minutes. Remove pan from heat and stir in herbs, zest, lemon juice, and salt.

Meanwhile, cook pasta in a pot of boiling salted water until al dente. Reserve 3 tablespoons of pasta-cooking water, before draining pasta.

Toss pasta with crab sauce and reserved cooking water in a serving bowl. Season with salt and pepper. Top with grated Parmesan cheese, if desired.

Suggested wine: Chablis

Fettuccine with Creamy Red Pepper Sauce

Serves 4 to 6

2 tablespoons olive oil

I small onion, chopped

3 garlic cloves, chopped

I (16-ounce) jar of roasted red peppers, drained and chopped

$^1/_2$ cup chicken stock

I cup feta cheese, crumbled

I pound whole wheat fettuccine

Salt and pepper to taste

Heat the olive oil over medium high heat. Sauté the onions and garlic for approximately 10 minutes. Add the roasted red peppers and sauté until heated through. Remove from heat and cool slightly.

Place mixture in a food processor with the chicken stock and feta cheese. Blend until combined and smooth.

Cook pasta and drain. Toss the pasta with the sauce. Adjust seasonings. Sprinkle with additional feta cheese.

Suggested wine: Chianti

Recipe Notes

Recipe Notes

End of Summer Roasted Vegetables on Pasta

Serves 12

¹/₂ cup olive oil

8 garlic cloves

1³/₄ pounds ripe plum tomatoes, seeded and chopped

2 medium zucchinis, cut into thin matchsticks

2 medium green bell peppers, cut into thin strips

1 medium yellow bell pepper, cut into thin strips

1 medium red bell pepper, cut into thin strips

1 pound rotelle pasta

8 large scallions, thinly sliced through 2 inches of green

1¹/₂ cups basil, coarsely chopped

1 teaspoon salt

1 teaspoon pepper

1 cup freshly grated Parmesan cheese

Preheat oven to 375°F. In a large casserole or baking dish combine the olive oil and garlic cloves. Bake for 10 minutes, until garlic is golden. Remove from oven, using a slotted spoon, discard garlic. Add to dish the tomatoes, zucchini and peppers. Toss well and return to the oven and bake for 10 minutes or until vegetables are slightly softened.

In a large pot of salted water cook pasta until al dente. Drain and add to the casserole. Add scallions, basil, salt, pepper and Parmesan cheese. Toss very well. Serve warm or cold. Can be topped with additional Parmesan cheese.

Pasta with Olives, Tomatoes and Cheese

Serves 4

6 tablespoons olive oil

1½ cups onion, chopped

1 teaspoon garlic, minced

3 cans (28 ounce) Italian plum tomatoes, drained

2½ teaspoons dried basil

1 teaspoon crushed red pepper

2 cups chicken or vegetable broth

1 pound penne pasta

3 cups Havarti cheese, grated or chopped

⅓ cup Kalamata olives, pitted and sliced

½ cup Parmesan cheese, grated

Heat oil in large heavy pan on medium high heat. Sauté onion and garlic until translucent, about 6 minutes. Add tomatoes, basil and crushed red pepper. Bring to a boil and break up the tomatoes, a wooden spoon works well. Add the broth and bring back to a boil, then reduce to simmer until mixture thickens to chunky sauce. This takes about an hour and you need to stir occasionally.

Preheat oven to 375°F. Cook the pasta in boiling water until al dente. Drain and return to the same pot. Mix with the sauce, adding the Havarti cheese and olives. Place in 9x13-inch in baking dish and sprinkle with Parmesan cheese. Bake until heated, which takes about 30 minutes.

For a nice addition, include cooked chicken in this dish.

Suggested wine: Chianti

Recipe Notes

Recipe Notes

Italian Ragu over Pasta

Serves 8 to 10

4 tablespoons butter

4 tablespoons olive oil

3 onions, finely chopped

2 carrots, finely diced

1½ stalks celery, chopped

¼ pound pancetta, finely diced

1 pound ground beef

¾ pound ground pork

6 large chicken livers

½ cup dry white wine

3 cups chicken or beef stock

½ cup tomato purée

½ pound mushrooms

1 clove garlic, finely chopped

3 tablespoons parsley, finely chopped

1 cup heavy cream

Heat olive oil with the butter. Sauté onions, carrots, celery and pancetta until golden. Add the meats gradually, breaking them into small pieces. Cook until meats render their fats and turn brown. Add white wine and let it evaporate on high heat. Add stock, stir well. Bring to simmer and add tomato purée. Add pinch of salt and pepper and simmer for 1½ hours.

Meanwhile, sauté mushrooms in remaining butter, adding pinch of salt and pepper. Add garlic and chopped parsley. When sauce is done simmering, add mushrooms and heavy cream. Simmer together for about 5 minutes to blend the flavors and serve over pasta.

Traditionally, this sauce is served over ravioli, however, the sauce is very rich and works well over rigatoni pasta.

Suggested wine: Barbaresco

Desserts

Desserts

Classic Apple Pan Dowdy

Serves 4 to 6

I cup flour

I cup sugar

I teaspoon baking powder

I egg, beaten

4 apples, peeled, sliced

$^1/_2$ stick butter, melted

Brown sugar to taste

Cinnamon to taste

Sift flour, sugar and baking powder together into a bowl. Add the egg, stirring until crumbly. Place apples in 8-inch square baking pan. Sprinkle with brown sugar and cinnamon. Spoon flour mixture over the top. Drizzle with butter. Bake at 350°F for 35 minutes. Serve warm.

Patriotic Parfait

Serves 4

3 ounces good quality white chocolate, broken into pieces

I cup heavy cream

2 tablespoons sugar

3 ounces cream cheese, softened

I cup strawberries, sliced (may use raspberries, or both)

I cup blueberries (large high bush berries are prettier)

Melt chocolate and set aside. Beat cream in medium bowl until soft peaks form. Slowly add sugar, beat until stiff peaks form. Transfer to a medium bowl and set aside. In original mixing bowl, beat cream cheese until fluffy. Add chocolate in a stream while beating; beat until smooth. Stir in ¼ of the whipped cream. Gently fold in remaining whipped cream.

In parfait glasses, alternately layer mousse and mixed berries. Parfait may be served immediately or refrigerated up to 6 hours.

Garnish with sliced strawberries, raspberries and blueberries. Perfect for July 4th celebration!

Recipe Notes

Baked Pears with Butterscotch Sauce

Serves 6

6 medium ripe but firm Bosc pears, peeled and halved lengthwise

6 tablespoons unsalted butter

¹/₂ cup golden brown sugar, packed

¹/₈ teaspoon salt

3 tablespoons Scotch

I teaspoon vanilla

3 tablespoons heavy cream

Preheat oven to 350°F. Cut pears in half and scoop out core from each pear half. Melt butter in large ovenproof skillet over medium heat. Whisk in brown sugar and salt. Arrange pears, cut side down, in large skillet in single layer. Spoon some of the sugar mixture over pears. Place skillet in oven and bake pears until tender, basting once with syrup, about 30 minutes. Transfer pears to large plate. Carefully place skillet on stove top and add Scotch and vanilla to the syrup that is remaining in the skillet. Cook over medium high heat (be careful because syrup may ignite). Cook until syrup is reduced by half, whisking often, about 2 minutes. When syrup has been reduced, add heavy cream. Spoon syrup over pears and serve. Use any remaining syrup over ice cream.

Kahlúa Mousse

Serves 10

I pound dark sweetened chocolate

2 tablespoons butter

¹/₂ cup powdered sugar, sifted

3 eggs, separated

¹/₄ cup Kahlúa

I teaspoon powdered instant coffee

2 cups heavy cream

Melt chocolate and butter over low heat. In a large bowl, beat the sugar, egg yolks, liqueur and coffee. Stir in the melted chocolate. Whip the cream to stiff peaks. Fold into the chocolate mixture. Beat egg whites to soft peaks. Fold into mousse. Pour into a serving bowl or individual goblets. Chill overnight. Garnish with whipped cream and shaved chocolate.

Caramel Popcorn

¹/₂ cup salted butter

¹/₂ cup margarine

2 cups brown sugar

¹/₂ cup corn syrup

I teaspoon salt

¹/₂ teaspoon baking soda

I teaspoon vanilla

3 bags popcorn popped in microwave (light popcorn)

Preheat oven to 250°F. Melt margarine and butter together. Stir in brown sugar, corn syrup and salt. Bring to a hard boil. Boil for 5 minutes without stirring. Remove from the heat and stir in baking soda and vanilla. Place popped popcorn in a bowl. Pour syrup over popcorn and stir until popcorn is well coated. Place in two large shallow baking dishes and bake for 45 minutes, stirring every 15 minutes. Allow to cool completely. Place in airtight containers for storage until ready to serve.

Great to take to the mountain to munch on after skiing!

Recipe Notes

Chocolate Scotchies

Serves 4

I cup chocolate chips

I cup butterscotch chips

I cup cocktail peanuts

I cup chow mein noodles

Melt chips in double boiler until melted. Remove from heat. Stir in peanuts and noodles. Scoop onto cookie sheets (tablespoon size). Freeze for 15 minutes. Ready to eat! Keep cool.

These are an easy introduction to cooking for youngsters; fun to make on an inclement day with fairly instant gratification!

Chocolate Krinkles

Makes 3 dozen

$^1/_2$ cup vegetable oil

4 squares unsweetened chocolate, melted

2 cups sugar

4 eggs

2 teaspoons vanilla

2 cups flour

2 teaspoons baking powder

$^1/_2$ teaspoon salt

Powdered sugar

Mix oil, chocolate and sugar. Add eggs and vanilla. Mix dry ingredients and add to batter. Chill several hours or overnight. Roll a heaping teaspoonful of batter into a ball, then roll in sugar. Bake at 350°F for 10 to 12 minutes. Be careful not to over bake.

These are good anytime—but a great addition to your holiday cookie assortment.

Nana Goldstein's Raspberry Bars

A Dozen Large Bars

2¹/₂ cups flour

I cup sugar

I cup chopped pecans

I cup butter

I egg

I jar (16 ounce) raspberry jam

Preheat oven to 350°F. Mix all ingredients, except jam, together until crumbly. Spread ¾ of mixture in a 9 x 11-inch pan. Spread jam on top. Sprinkle with remaining mixture. Bake for 45 minutes.

These are easy and everyone loves them. Wrap and take to the beach!

Honey Bars

Serves 9

¹/₂ cup sugar

¹/₂ cup solid vegetable shortening

¹/₂ cup Maine honey

I egg

²/₃ cup sifted flour

I cup coconut, finely chopped

I cup rolled oats

¹/₂ teaspoon baking powder

I teaspoon vanilla

Mix all ingredients and spread in buttered 9-inch square pan. Bake at 350°F for 30 to 35 minutes. While warm, cut in to squares.

Great lunch box snack! A favorite since the recipe appeared in my third grade mimeographed cookbook!

Recipe Notes

Recipe Notes

White Chocolate Macadamia Coconut Squares

2 dozen small squares

CRUST

2¹/₃ cups flour, spooned in and leveled

²/₃ cup sifted powdered sugar, spooned in and leveled

¹/₂ teaspoon salt

³/₄ cup (I¹/₂ sticks) unsalted butter, cold, cut into ¹/₂-inch cubes

Preheat oven to 350°F. Tear off a sheet of heavy-duty aluminum foil measuring 18x16-inch. Invert a 9x13-inch metal pan and center the foil over the pan, pressing it across the bottom and down the sides. Remove the foil, turn the pan right side up and place the foil into the pan, shaping it smooth and tight against the sides. Gently butter foil. Combine the flour, sugar and salt in the bowl of a food processor and pulse several times to blend. Add the butter and process until a smooth dough forms. Distribute dough evenly in pan and press uniformly into the bottom of the pan. Bake the crust for about 25 minutes until nicely golden. Crust will pull away from edges of pan.

TOPPING

I cup plus 2 tablespoons sugar

I cup heavy cream

¹/₄ cup (¹/₂ stick) unsalted butter, melted

I tablespoon fresh lemon juice, strained

I¹/₂ teaspoons vanilla

¹/₂ teaspoon salt

3 cups (about 9 ounces) sweetened flaked coconut, lightly packed

2¹/₂ cups salted macadamia nuts, halved and toasted at 350°F until golden (about 5 minutes, watch carefully so as not to burn)

8 - 9 ounces white chocolate chips or chopped white chocolate

White Chocolate Macadamia Coconut Squares — continued

Reduce the oven temperature to 325°F. Combine the sugar, heavy cream, melted butter, lemon juice, vanilla and salt in large bowl. Add the coconut, nuts and chocolate, stirring until the ingredients are coated with the sugar/cream mixture. Empty the topping over the hot crust and smooth in with the back of a spoon. Bake for 40 to 50 minutes until the topping has flattened, stopped bubbling and is lightly browned. At first it will puff up and then settle. Remove pan from oven and set on a rack to cool to room temperature, then cover with foil and refrigerate for several hours to get cold. Holding the foil, lift the bar out of the pan. You may need to release the side with a knife to loosen. While bar is still chilled, trim the hard edges and cut into small squares. Refrigerate or freeze in an airtight container, layered between wax paper.

Pecan Snowballs

7 to 8 dozen

1 cup unsalted, softened butter	1 teaspoon salt
³/₄ cup shortening	4 cups flour
1¹/₄ cups powdered sugar	1 cup pecans, ground
2 tablespoons vanilla	

In a large mixing bowl using paddle attachment, cream butter, shortening, sugar, vanilla and salt together. Scrape the bowl frequently so there are no lumps. In a separate bowl, mix the flour and the pecans together. Add flour mixture to the butter mixture and continue mixing until well incorporated.

Scoop or shape dough by hand into balls—approximately 1-inch in diameter. Bake in a 350°F oven until slightly golden brown. After baking, roll in powdered sugar and then roll again once completely cooled.

Add to your holiday cookie list!

Recipe Notes

Luscious Lemon Bars

Serves 12

When served as dessert: Sometimes I put a lemon square on a plate and serve with grated chocolate and powdered sugar shaken over the bar and the plate, and sometimes I add a chocolate leaf or two. In the summer, I often put fresh berries on top of the bar or next to it on the plate, perhaps with mint leaves or a summer flower. Another presentation is to purée some raspberries and serve the bar on top of a raspberry coulis, perhaps with a few blueberries on top. Another idea is to shake toasted pistachios (chopped) over the bar or toasted coconut shards. Perhaps put a nasturtium or two on the plate.

CRUST

1 1/2 cups flour

1/2 cup powdered sugar

1 1/2 sticks cold, unsalted butter

Preheat oven to 325°F. Mix all 3 ingredients in food processor until consistency is like cornmeal. Press on bottom and slightly up the sides of 9x13-inch metal pan. Bake for 20 to 25 minutes. Turn oven down to 300°F.

FILLING

6 eggs

3 cups sugar

1 cup plus 2 tablespoons fresh lemon juice (about 6 to 8 lemons)

1/2 cup flour, added slowly with whisk to blend thoroughly

Mix together all ingredients and pour mixture onto crust (it is not necessary for crust to be cool). Bake at 300°F for 40 minutes or until set.

To serve...cut as cookies or use as dessert (3x3-inch is a good size). Must be COLD before cutting to get a clean edge. Freezes well in airtight container.

Turtle Bars

Makes about 70, 1-inch squares

CRUST
2 cups flour

I cup dark brown sugar, packed

³/₄ cup unsalted butter, (I¹/₂ sticks) room temperature

Preheat oven to 350°F. Mix flour, brown sugar and butter in food processor until well blended and crumbly. Press mixture evenly into ungreased 9x13-inch metal non-stick baking dish. Bake until crust is light golden, about 15 minutes. Maintain oven temperature.

FILLING
I¹/₂ cups pecan pieces (can use halves or pieces)

³/₄ cup unsalted butter (I¹/₂ sticks)

3 tablespoons whipping cream

³/₄ cup dark brown sugar, packed

While crust is baking, bring brown sugar, butter and cream to a boil in a small saucepan over high heat, stirring until sugar dissolves. Boil 1 minute, stirring occasionally. Remove from heat. Sprinkle pecans over crust. Pour caramel filling over pecans. Bake until bubbles form and color darkens, about 20 minutes.

TOPPING
I cup semisweet chocolate chips (add a few more if you think you need them)

Remove from oven and sprinkle with chocolate chips. Let stand until chocolate melts, about 5 minutes, and then spread the chocolate evenly over top. Chill bars until chocolate sets, about 20 minutes. Cut into 1-inch squares.

Recipe Notes

Chocolate Espresso Pudding

4 servings

¹/₂ cup packed brown sugar

¹/₄ cup cornstarch

3 tablespoons unsweetened cocoa (highest quality you can find)

1 tablespoon instant coffee granules

¹/₈ teaspoon salt

2 cups fat-free soy milk

2 ounces bittersweet chocolate, chopped (highest quality you can find)

1 teaspoon vanilla

Combine first 5 ingredients in a heavy medium saucepan, and stir well with a whisk. Gradually stir in milk and bring to a boil over medium heat. Reduce heat, and simmer 1 minute or until thick. Remove from heat and add chocolate, stirring until melted. Stir in vanilla. Pour about ½ cup pudding into each of 4 dessert dishes; cover surface of pudding with plastic wrap. Chill at least 4 hours. Remove plastic wrap to serve.

Can be served with whipped cream, topped with chocolate shavings.

Lemon Sponge Custard

Serves 4 to 6

³/₄ cup sugar

1¹/₂ tablespoons butter

2 teaspoons lemon rind, grated

2 eggs, separated

3 tablespoons flour

¹/₄ cup lemon juice

I cup milk

Preheat oven to 350°F. Cream sugar and butter with lemon rind. Add egg yolks and beat well. Stir in flour alternately with lemon juice and milk. Beat egg whites until stiff but not dry and fold them into the yolk mixture. Place batter in buttered custard cups or a 7-inch ovenproof dish. Set on a rack in a pan filled with 1-inch of hot water. Bake 45 minutes for cups, 1 hour for dish, or until set. Serve cold or warm with fresh berries.

Recipe Notes

Banana Bread Pudding with Caramel Sauce

Serves 4

²/₃ cup low-fat milk

2 tablespoons dark brown sugar

4 tablespoons sugar, divided

¹/₄ teaspoon cinnamon

1 cup ripe mashed banana (about 2), divided

2 large eggs

Powdered sugar

Caramel sauce

4 cups French bread cut into ¹/₂-inch cubes (4 slices), divided

Vegetable cooking spray

Preheat oven to 350°F. Combine milk, sugars and cinnamon in small bowl. Stir with a whisk. Place ½ cup bread cubes into each of 4 (8 ounce) ramekins coated with cooking spray. Spoon 2 tablespoons of the milk mixture over each serving and top with ¼ cup banana. Sprinkle each serving with 1½ teaspoons sugar. Repeat procedure with remaining bread and milk mixture. Chill 30 minutes. Bake for 50 minutes or until done. Spoon 1 tablespoon caramel sauce over each, sprinkle with powdered sugar.

Serve warm—perfect for winter evenings around the fire.

Chocolate Croissant Bread Pudding

Serves 12 or more

I stick unsalted butter	5 large eggs, lightly beaten
I cup sugar	2¹/₂ cups heavy cream
2 teaspoons ground cinnamon	I2 large croissants
I¹/₂ teaspoons vanilla	³/₄ cup chopped bittersweet chocolate

Preheat oven to 350°F. Cream butter and sugar until well blended. Add cinnamon and vanilla and blend well. Beat in the eggs. Add cream to combine. (All of this may be done in a food processor.)

Lightly butter a 9x13-inch baking dish. Break up croissants into 1-inch pieces and layer in the pan. Scatter chocolate over the top and gently mix to incorporate (layering may make this easier). Pour the egg mixture over the top and soak for 8 to 10 minutes. Push the croissant pieces down to ensure coverage by the egg mixture.

Cover with foil and bake for 35 minutes. Remove foil and bake for an additional 10 minutes to brown the top. The pudding is done when the custard is set, but still soft. May be served cold or warm (though must cool somewhat before serving).

Good topped with whipped cream or mocha or vanilla ice cream. A favorite of both the soccer and ski teams!

Recipe Notes

Chocolate Truffle Loaf with Raspberry Sauce

Serves 12

2 packages (8 ounce) semisweet chocolate squares, coarsely chopped

¹/₂ cup butter

⁵/₆ cup light corn syrup, divided

2 cups heavy whipping cream, divided

3 large egg yolks

¹/₄ cup powdered sugar

I teaspoon vanilla

I package (I2 ounce) frozen raspberries, partially thawed

Line a 9 x 5-inch loaf pan with plastic wrap. Set aside. Melt chocolate, butter, and ½ cup corn syrup in a heavy saucepan over medium-low heat, stirring until smooth. Whisk together ½ cup whipping cream and egg yolks in a small bowl. Gradually stir into chocolate mixture, whisking constantly. Cook over medium-low heat 5 minutes. Remove from heat, and let cool 45 minutes or until mixture reaches room temperature.

Beat remaining 1½ cups whipping cream, powdered sugar, and vanilla at high speed with an electric mixer until soft peaks form. Gently fold into chocolate mixture until no white streaks remain. Pour chocolate mixture into prepared pan. Cover and freeze 3 hours or until firm.

Process raspberries and ⅓ cup corn syrup in a blender until smooth, stopping to scrape down sides. Cover and chill until ready to serve.

Gently invert loaf pan onto a serving platter; remove pan and plastic wrap. Slice chocolate loaf into 12 servings, spread a small amount of raspberry sauce on a plate and lay slice on top. Garnish with fresh raspberries if desired.

This is actually a very easy recipe to make that presents beautifully. Both loaf and sauce can be made the day before. Fresh mint leaves can be added to the fresh raspberry garnish.

Rosie's Trifle

Serves 12

12-24 ladyfingers, split

18-24 coconut macaroon cookies, crumbled and divided

Jam, your favorite strawberry

1 cup whipping cream

1/4 cup sugar

1 teaspoon vanilla

Fresh strawberries to garnish

Sherry

Rum

Line trifle dish (or other glass or crystal serving bowl) with ladyfingers or cake slices. Sprinkle with sherry and rum. Layer half the crumbled macaroon cookies. Sprinkle with sherry and rum.

VANILLA PUDDING *(you may use packaged pudding mix to save time!)*

1 1/3 cups sugar

1/2 cup cornstarch

1 teaspoon salt

6 cups milk

8 egg yolks, slightly beaten

4 tablespoons butter, softened

2 tablespoons plus 2 teaspoons vanilla

Stir sugar and cornstarch and salt together in a large saucepan. Mix milk with slightly beaten egg yolks. Stir into sugar mixture. Heat slowly to boiling, then boil 1 minute. Remove from heat, add butter and vanilla. Cover with plastic wrap and let cool. Add a little sherry and pour into trifle bowl over layer of macaroon cookies. Layer more ladyfingers, spread a thin layer of jam, sprinkle sherry, rum and the remaining macaroons. Whip cream, gradually adding sugar until soft peaks form. Stir in vanilla. Cover trifle with whipped cream. Top with fresh strawberries.

My mom, Rose, always hid this from the kids, until the guests were served!

Recipe Notes

Chocolate Almond Torte

Serves 12

Recipe Notes

1½ cups blanched slivered almonds

1 cup sugar, divided

8 ounces semisweet (not unsweetened) or bittersweet chocolate, chopped

5 large eggs, separated

½ teaspoon almond extract

½ teaspoon lemon peel, grated

½ cup (1 stick) unsalted butter, melted, cooled

¼ teaspoon salt

Powdered sugar

Preheat oven to 350°F. Butter 10-inch springform pan with 2¾-inch high sides. Combine almonds and ⅓ cup sugar in processor. Blend until almonds are very finely ground. Transfer almond mixture to medium bowl, do not clean processor. Add chocolate and ⅓ cup sugar to processor. Blend until chocolate is finely ground but not beginning to clump, about 45 seconds. Stir in to almond mixture. Using an electric mixer, beat egg yolks and remaining ⅓ cup sugar in large bowl until mixture falls in heavy ribbon when beaters are lifted, about 5 minutes. Beat in almond extract and lemon peel. Fold in chocolate/almond mixture, then butter. (Mixture will be thick.)

Using clean, dry beaters, beat egg whites and salt in another large bowl until stiff, but not dry. Fold whites into chocolate batter in three additions. Transfer batter to prepared pan. Bake cake until tester inserted comes out with some moist crumbs attached, about 40 minutes. Cool cake completely in pan on rack. (Cover; store at room temperature.) Cut around side of pan to loosen, release sides. Sift powdered sugar over cake.

Best when eaten the day it is made.

Great with fresh raspberries on the side.

Raspberry Fudge Brownies

Makes 32

1 package (10-ounce) frozen raspberries in light syrup, thawed and undrained

1/4 cup plus 2 tablespoons unsalted margarine

1/4 cup plus 2 tablespoons unsweetened cocoa

2/3 cup sugar

2 eggs, beaten

1/2 teaspoon vanilla

1/2 cup flour

1/8 teaspoon salt

Vegetable cooking spray

Preheat oven to 350°F. Drain raspberries, reserving 3 tablespoons juice. Set raspberries and juice aside. Combine margarine and cocoa in a large saucepan. Cook over low heat, stirring constantly, until margarine melts and mixture becomes smooth. Remove from heat; let cool slightly. Add sugar, eggs and vanilla to cocoa mixture, stirring well to combine. Stir in 3 tablespoons reserved raspberry juice. Combine flour and salt; add flour mixture to cocoa mixture, stirring well to combine. Gently fold raspberries into cocoa mixture.

Spoon batter into an 8-inch square baking pan that has been coated with cooking spray. Bake for 20 minutes or until a wooden pick inserted in center comes out clean. Let brownies cool completely; cut into 2-inch squares. Cut squares in half to form triangles.

Nothing much better than chocolate and raspberries! Try with frozen vanilla yogurt or ice cream.

Recipe Notes

Recipe Notes

Vicky's Special Brownies with Frosting

Serves 12

7 squares unsweetened chocolate, divided

$^2/_3$ cup plus **2** tablespoons butter, divided

2 cups sugar

I teaspoon baking powder

I teaspoon salt

I$^1/_4$ cups sifted flour

2 eggs

2 teaspoons vanilla, divided

$^1/_4$ teaspoon salt

2 cups powdered sugar

$^1/_3$ cup milk

Preheat oven to 350°F. Melt 4 squares chocolate with ⅔ cup butter. Sift together all dry ingredients. Add eggs and 1 teaspoon vanilla. Mix in chocolate and butter mixture. Bake 30 minutes in greased 13x9-inch pan. For frosting, melt 2 tablespoons butter with 3 squares unsweetened chocolate. Gradually add powdered sugar, milk, remaining teaspoon of vanilla, and salt. Let brownies cool slightly before frosting.

My stepmother made these for every special occasion when we were growing up, hence the name. They are quite rich and you may want to cut into smaller squares. Great for a picnic.

Chocolate Zucchini Nut Bread

2 Loaves

2 cups zucchini, shredded

2 ounces unsweetened chocolate, melted

3 cups flour

I teaspoon salt

I teaspoon cinnamon

I teaspoon baking soda

$^1/_2$ teaspoon baking powder

3 eggs

2 cups sugar

I cup vegetable oil

I teaspoon vanilla

I cup chopped nuts

Combine dry ingredients in a large bowl. In a separate bowl, beat eggs well. Add sugar, continue beating. Add oil and vanilla, mix well. Mix in melted chocolate. Pour over dry ingredients and stir. Add nuts. Fold in zucchini. Divide into 2 greased loaf pans. Bake at 350°F for 1 hour and 20 minutes. Cooking time varies greatly with oven. Test when loaf cracks, knife should come out clean.

Freeze ahead for summer guests. Great picnic fare!

Recipe Notes

Cream Puffs

Serves 16

Recipe Notes

PUFFS

I cup flour	I cup water
$^{1}/_{4}$ teaspoon salt	4 eggs
$^{1}/_{2}$ cup shortening	

Blend dry ingredients. Add shortening to water and bring to a boil. Add dry ingredients all at once. Beat constantly until mixture leaves the sides of pan and forms a ball. Remove from heat and cool slightly. Add eggs, one at a time. Beat until smooth after each. Drop by tablespoonful onto ungreased baking sheet. Bake at 400°F for 40 to 45 minutes. Cool thoroughly. Remove tops, fill with cream filling, replace tops, sprinkle with powdered sugar.

CREAM FILLING

2 cups milk	Dash of salt
$^{1}/_{2}$ cup sugar	3 egg yolks
2 heaping tablespoons flour	I teaspoon vanilla

Over low heat stir milk, sugar, flour and salt. Add egg yolks one at a time, stirring until thickened. Add vanilla. Cool and fill puffs just before serving. Sprinkle with powdered sugar.

Of course, you may make packaged pudding, though this is easy to do! If preparing ahead, cover cream filling with plastic wrap and store in the refrigerator. Do NOT fill puffs until ready to serve, as they may get soggy!

May fill with ice cream and top with chocolate sauce.

Cream Puffs — continued

BLUE RIBBON CHOCOLATE SAUCE

1/2 cup butter	I box powdered sugar
4 ounces unsweetened chocolate	I can evaporated milk

Melt chocolate and butter in top of a double boiler. Remove from heat. Add powdered sugar alternatively with milk. Mix well after each addition. Return to heat and cook in double boiler for 30 minutes.

Store in refrigerator for several weeks or may be frozen. When ready to use, heat in double boiler and, if necessary, add a little water.

Rhubarb Cream Pie

Serves 8

I unbaked 9-inch pie crust	I1/3 cups sugar
I1/2 cups fresh or frozen, but thawed rhubarb, cut into 1/2-inch pieces	Dash cinnamon
	Dash nutmeg
3 tablespoons flour	2 eggs
	I cup heavy cream

Preheat oven to 350°F. Mix flour and sugar together. Toss together with the rhubarb, cinnamon and nutmeg and set aside. Beat eggs. Add cream. Blend with rhubarb mixture and pour into pie shell. Bake until golden brown and knife comes out clean, about 40 to 45 minutes. Great topped with vanilla ice cream, but not necessary.

Every garden in Maine seems to have this favorite perennial making an early appearance in the spring. If rhubarb doesn't grow in your garden, you can find it in the produce department, or, if out of season, the frozen version will do.

Recipe Notes

Rhubarb Crisp

Serves 9

FILLING

4 cups rhubarb cut into $^1/_2$-inch pieces

$^3/_4$ cup white sugar

$^3/_4$ cup packed brown sugar

3 tablespoons flour

1 tablespoon lemon juice

2 eggs, beaten

1 tablespoon butter

Combine sugar, flour, lemon juice, eggs and butter. Mix well. Mix in rhubarb, pour in 8x8 or 9-inch pie plate.

TOPPING

$^3/_4$ cup sugar

$^1/_2$ cup flour

2 teaspoons orange rind, grated

$^1/_3$ cup butter, softened

Mix all ingredients until. Sprinkle over filling. Bake 375°F for 45 to 50 minutes until golden.

Freeze cubed rhubarb on cookie sheets—once frozen put in freezer bags. A great way to enjoy summer in the middle of winter

This is our "here comes summer" dessert—serve warm with vanilla ice cream.

Veda's Whoopie Pies

12 small pies

CAKES

¹/₂ cup solid vegetable shortening	2 cups flour
I cup sugar	¹/₂ teaspoon baking soda
I egg	I pinch salt
I cup milk	¹/₂ cup cocoa
I teaspoon vanilla	

Preheat oven to 425°F. Cream the shortening, then add the rest of the ingredients in order. Drop 24 spoonfuls on an ungreased cookie sheet. Bake about 7 minutes.

FILLING

³/₄ cup confectioners' sugar	³/₈ cup solid vegetable shortening
¹/₂ cup marshmallow creme	³/₈ cup butter, softened

Mix and spread on cool cakes, layering one on top to make a sandwich.

If you are like me and love plenty of frosting in your whoopie pies, I would recommend doubling the amount of filling.

This is a very popular Maine treat!

Recipe Notes

Pumpkin Whoopie Pies

12 small pies

PIES

I cup solid vegetable shortening

I cup sugar

I can (15 ounce) pumpkin

I egg

2 cups flour

I teaspoon baking soda

I teaspoon cinnamon

$^1/_2$ cup raisins (optional)

$^1/_2$ cup chopped walnuts (optional)

Cream together shortening, sugar and pumpkin. Add egg and mix. Blend in flour, baking soda and cinnamon. Add raisins and walnuts if desired. Drop by tablespoons on greased baking sheet. Bake at 350°F for 10 to 12 minutes.

FROSTING

I can white frosting

I package (8 ounce) cream cheese

Whip frosting and cream cheese together. When "pies" have cooled, generously layer frosting between 2 pies.

The dough can be scooped into 1-inch balls and these balls can be frozen (in an air tight container) until needed.

Recipe Notes

Grasshopper Pie

Serves 8

CRUST

1¼ cups crushed chocolate wafers   4 tablespoons butter, melted

Combine crushed wafers with butter (reserving some to sprinkle on top of pie). Press mixture evenly into 9-inch pan. Freeze for 1 hour. (Alternatively, can use purchased pre-made chocolate crust).

FILLING

20 large marshmallows

2 cups whipping cream, divided

4 tablespoons green crème de menthe

Combine marshmallows and 1 cup cream in heavy pan. Heat slowly and stir until marshmallows are melted. When mixture is cool, whip remaining cup cream and fold whipped cream into mixture. Add crème de menthe and mix well. Pour into shell and sprinkle some crushed cookies on top. Return to freezer for at least 2 hours.

Refreshing and minty, and of course perfect when looking for something green for St. Patrick's Day dessert!

Sour Cream Apple Pie

Serves 8

PIE CRUST

1¹/₂ cups flour

¹/₂ teaspoon salt

I teaspoon cinnamon

¹/₂ cup shortening

4 - 5 tablespoons apple juice

Sift flour, cinnamon and salt into bowl. Add shortening. Cut in with pastry-blender or blending fork until the pieces are the size of small peas. Add apple juice by teaspoonful, tossing with a fork until all the flour-coated bits of shortening are barely dampened. Stop! Turn mixture onto a square of waxed paper. Gather up corners, pressing from the outside to form a compact ball. Chill for easier handling. When ready to bake pie, roll out and crimp sides.

FILLING

8 apples, peeled and thinly sliced

¹/₃ cup flour

I egg, beaten

I²/₃ cups sour cream

2 teaspoons vanilla

I cup sugar

Preheat oven to 450°F. Combine apples, flour, egg, sour cream, vanilla and sugar. Spoon into the prepared crust and bake 10 minutes. Reduce heat to 350°F and continue baking for 40 minutes more.

TOPPING

¹/₃ cup sugar

I cup chopped walnuts

¹/₂ cup flour

¹/₃ cup brown sugar

I tablespoon cinnamon

I stick butter

Pinch of salt

While pie is baking, mix all of the topping ingredients until crumbly. Spoon over pie and bake 15 minutes longer.

Cranberry Pake

Serves 8

1½ cups sugar, divided

2½ cups fresh cranberries

½ cup chopped walnuts

¾ cup butter

½ teaspoon vanilla

2 eggs, beaten

1 (10-inch) pie crust, unbaked

Preheat oven to 350°F. Line a 10-inch pie plate with your favorite pastry recipe. Mix cranberries, 1/2 cup sugar and walnuts. Place in prepared crust. Cream butter and remaining sugar. Add vanilla and eggs. Mix in flour. Batter will be very thick, use a strong spatula to spread over cranberry mixture into pie shell. Be sure to have filling touch sides of the shell to seal. Bake for 1 hour. Serve warm or cold with a dollop of whipped cream.

Colorful dessert, great for a holiday dessert buffet!

Recipe Notes

Recipe Notes

Crustless Chocolate Mousse Pie

Serves 8

8 eggs, separated

Dash salt

2 tablespoons brandy, bourbon or rum

4 ounces unsweetened chocolate, melted and cooled

$^1/_2$ cup heavy cream

1 cup sugar

Grease 9-inch pie pan or spring form pan. In a large bowl, beat egg whites until stiff but not dry. In a small bowl, beat egg yolks, salt and brandy. Add sugar gradually and beat at high speed until thick and light colored. Add chocolate. Fold chocolate mixture into egg whites. Pour half the mixture into pan and bake at 350°F for 18 to 20 minutes until slightly moist in the center. Cool. Whip cream and fold in remaining chocolate mixture. Spoon onto cooled, baked mousse and chill several hours. Serve with more whipped cream.

Hugs and Kisses Cheese Pie

Serves 8

1 pre-packaged chocolate cookie pie crust	1 egg
	1 teaspoon vanilla
2 packages (3 ounce) cream cheese, softened	1 cup mini or regular chocolate chips
1 can (14 ounce) condensed milk	1 teaspoon flour

Preheat oven to 350°F. With mixer, beat cream cheese until fluffy. Gradually beat in condensed milk until smooth. Add egg and vanilla. Toss chocolate chips with flour and stir into cheese mixture. Pour into pie crust. Bake 35 minutes or until center springs back.

GLAZE

½ cup chocolate chips	¼ cup whipping cream

While pie is baking melt chocolate chips with whipping cream. Cook and stir until thickened and smooth. Keep stirring so the chocolate does not burn. Do not boil. Immediately spread over pie, refrigerate. Pie can also be made ahead of time and frozen.

Recipe Notes

Recipe Notes

Marble Cheesecake Squares

Serves 12

1 cup chocolate graham cracker crumbs

Cooking spray

1 tablespoon butter, melted

2 blocks (8 ounce) fat-free cream cheese, softened

1 cup sugar

3 tablespoons flour

1 tablespoon vanilla

3 large egg whites

1 large egg

1 ounce semisweet chocolate

Preheat oven to 325°F. Place crumbs in a 9-inch square baking pan coated with cooking spray; drizzle with butter. Toss with a fork until moist. Press into bottom of pan. Bake 8 minutes; cool on a wire rack. (You may use a pre-made purchased crust to save time!)

Place cheese in a large bowl; beat with a mixer at high speed until smooth. Add sugar and flour; beat well. Add vanilla, egg whites and egg; beat until well blended. Pour cheese mixture into prepared pan.

Place chocolate in a small microwave-safe bowl; microwave at high 1½ minutes or until soft, stirring after 45 seconds (chocolate should not completely melt). Stir until smooth. Drop melted chocolate onto cheese mixture to form 9 mounds. Swirl chocolate into batter using the tip of a knife. Bake for 35 minutes or until almost set. Cool on a wire rack. Cover and chill at least 4 hours.

If you've forgotten to set out the cream cheese to soften, arrange the unwrapped blocks in a single layer in a large bowl and microwave at HIGH for 1 minute or until slightly soft.

Elyse's Italian Cheesecake

Serves 10

Recipe Notes

CRUST

I cup graham cracker crumbs

¹/₄ cup sugar

¹/₂ cup butter, melted

Mix together all ingredients and pat into bottom of a large springform pan (9 to 10-inch).

FILLING

6 tablespoons flour

1³/₄ cups sugar

Pinch cinnamon

3 pounds ricotta cheese

6 eggs

In bowl add flour, sugar and cinnamon to ricotta cheese. Blend with beater until mixed. Beat in eggs, one at a time. Pour over crust. Bake in preheated 350°F oven for 1 hour. Do NOT open oven door. Turn off oven, leave the cheesecake in for 1 more hour. Remove from oven. Let cool 1½ hours, let spring go and sit out 6 hours or overnight before serving.

Great with fresh Maine strawberries or blueberries!

Recipe Notes

Blueberry Peach Cake

Serves 8 to 12

PASTRY

I¹/₂ cups flour

¹/₂ cup sugar

I teaspoon baking powder

¹/₄ teaspoon salt

I stick (¹/₂ cup) cold unsalted butter, cut into ¹/₂-inch cubes

I large egg

I teaspoon vanilla

Pulse together flour, sugar, baking powder and salt in a food processor until combined. Add butter and pulse just until mixture resembles coarse meal with some small (pea-size) butter lumps. Add egg and vanilla and pulse just until dough clumps and begins to form a ball. Press dough onto bottom and evenly (about ¼-inch thick) all the way up side of 9 to 9½-inch springform pan with floured fingertips. Chill pastry in pan until firm, about 10 minutes. (Depending on pan size, you may only be able to spread dough up ½ the sides of pan.)

FILLING

¹/₂ cup sugar, divided

2 tablespoons flour

I tablespoon quick-cooking tapioca

2 pounds firm-ripe peaches (about 4), halved lengthwise, pitted, and each half cut lengthwise into fourths

I cup blueberries (¹/₂ pint)

I tablespoon fresh lemon juice

While the pastry chills, grind 2 tablespoons sugar with flour and tapioca in food processor until tapioca is powdery, then transfer to a large bowl and stir in remaining 6 tablespoons sugar. Add peaches, blueberries, and lemon juice and gently toss to coat fruit. Spoon filling into pastry and bake, in preheated oven at 375°F, loosely covered with foil, until filling is bubbling in center and crust is golden, about 1³/₄ hours.

Experiment with other fruit combinations!

Apples and Cranberries

Plums and Blueberries

Mixed fruit combinations.

Blueberry Peach Cake — continued

Transfer cake in pan to a rack and cool, uncovered, 20 minutes. Carefully remove sides of pan. Cool cake to warm or room temperature, then cut into thick wedges with a sharp knife.

Cooking results are better when using a light-colored metal pan. Dark metal pans tend to brown baked goods more quickly. Pastry can be made and pressed in to pan 1 day ahead and chilled. Keep wrapped in plastic wrap. Remove from refrigerator 30 minutes before filling.

Hedy's Chocolate Cherry Cake

Serves 8

I can unsweetened cherries, drained	1/4 pound plus 3 tablespoons butter, softened
4 eggs, separated	6 ounces chocolate chips, melted
3/4 cup sugar	1/2 cup flour

Preheat oven to 350°F. Beat together egg yolks and sugar. Add the butter and mix. Stir in the chocolate. Mix in flour. Beat egg whites until stiff and fold in to batter. Spread gently into a buttered 9-inch springform pan. Place cherries on top. Bake for 40 to 50 minutes, or until knife comes out dry.

Serve with whipped cream or vanilla ice cream.

This is an old Austrian recipe, translated for American baking by my friend Hedy who brought it with her when she and her husband and son came to the U.S. to start a new life after World War II. It's a family birthday favorite.

Carrot Cake

Serves 10

CAKE

2 cups carrots, shredded

2 cups flour

2 cups sugar

4 eggs

1 teaspoon cinnamon

1 teaspoon baking soda

$^1/_2$ teaspoon baking powder

$1^1/_2$ cups vegetable oil

1 cup chopped walnuts

Using a sifter, mix the flour, sugar, cinnamon, baking soda and baking powder together. Add the carrots, oil and eggs and blend well. Add the walnuts. Grease an angel cake pan well. Bake the cake at 350°F for 50 to 60 minutes. Let cool and remove from pan. Place on decorative plate.

FROSTING

1 package (8 ounces) cream cheese, softened

$^1/_2$ stick butter, softened

$1^1/_2$ cups powdered sugar

Beat the cream cheese, butter and powdered sugar together. Add more sugar as needed to achieve a spreadable frosting. Frost the cake and serve.

This cake is very moist and worth the extra effort. You will never use a box mix again!

Recipe Notes

Mom's Chocolate Mayonnaise Cake with Mocha Frosting

Serves 10

CAKE

2 cups sifted flour

I cup sugar

4 tablespoons cocoa

I½ teaspoons baking soda

I½ teaspoons baking powder

I cup cold water

I cup mayonnaise-type salad dressing

2 teaspoons vanilla

Preheat oven to 350°F. Sift together dry ingredients. Add remaining ingredients and mix together thoroughly. Divide batter evenly between 2 lightly greased, floured round 8-inch cake pans. Bake 35 minutes or until done.

FROSTING

½ cup butter, creamed

I⅔ cups sifted powdered sugar

2 tablespoons cocoa

⅛ teaspoon salt

3 tablespoons strong hot coffee

I teaspoon vanilla

Gradually add sugar and cocoa to butter, blend until creamy. Add remaining ingredients and let stand 5 minutes. Beat well and then spread on cake. For generous frosting layer, double this amount.

Our favorite cake growing up, requested at every birthday. The mayonnaise makes it incredibly moist and the fresh coffee makes for a delicious mocha frosting.

Mint Chocolate Cake

Serves 8

Recipe Notes

1½ cups flour

1 cup sugar

3 tablespoons unsweetened cocoa

1 teaspoon baking soda

½ teaspoon salt

5 tablespoons butter, melted

1 tablespoon distilled white vinegar

1 teaspoon peppermint extract

1 cup cold water

1 cup semisweet chocolate minichips

½ cup walnuts, finely chopped (optional)

Preheat oven to 375°F. Into 8-inch springform pan, sift flour, sugar, cocoa, baking soda, and salt. With index finger, make 3 holes in flour mixture. Pour butter into one hole, vinegar into another, and peppermint extract into third hole. Pour water over all. With a fork, stir mixture until well combined. Bake cake 30 to 40 minutes or until cake tester inserted into center comes out clean. Immediately top cake with chocolate chips and bake 2 to 3 minutes longer, just until chips melt. With small spatula, loosen edge of cake and carefully remove from rim of pan. Spread melted chips evenly over top and sides of cake. With hand, gently pat walnuts around edge. Best if served same day made.

Best when using "mini" chocolate chips—they melt faster and are easier to spread.

Harvest Loaf Cake

Serves 8

CAKE

1³/₄ cups flour

I teaspoon baking soda

I teaspoon cinnamon

¹/₂ teaspoon salt

¹/₂ teaspoon nutmeg

¹/₄ teaspoon ginger

¹/₄ teaspoon cloves

¹/₂ cup butter

I cup sugar

2 eggs

³/₄ cup canned pumpkin

³/₄ cup chocolate chips

Preheat oven to 350°F. Combine flour with the baking soda, salt and spices. Beat the butter, adding the sugar and creaming well. Blend in the eggs, one at a time until blended. Add the dry ingredients, alternating with the pumpkin, beginning and ending with the dry ingredients. Stir in the chocolate chips. Grease or spray a 9 x 5-inch loaf pan. Pour the batter into the pan.

Bake for 60 to 75 minutes until wooden toothpick comes out clean. Cool slightly, remove from pan and put onto decorative dish. Pour glaze over the top.

SPICE GLAZE

¹/₂ cup powdered sugar

¹/₈ teaspoon nutmeg

¹/₈ teaspoon cinnamon

I - 2 tablespoons light cream

Mix together the sugar, nutmeg and cinnamon. Gradually add the cream to a thick, pouring consistency. Pour over the baked bread.

This cake reminds me of fall. We have served this as a bread at brunch or tea time.

Recipe Notes

Nana's Chocolate Applesauce Cake

Serves 9

2 cups flour, sifted

1 teaspoon cinnamon

$^1/_2$ teaspoon salt

$^1/_2$ cup cocoa

1 teaspoon ground cloves

$^2/_3$ cup solid vegetable shortening

1 cup sugar

2 cups unsweetened applesauce

2 teaspoons baking soda

1 cup raisins

Sift together flour, cinnamon, salt, cocoa and cloves. Cream together shortening and sugar. Heat applesauce and the baking soda. Add to the sugar and shortening mixture. When cool, add sifted ingredients. Fold in raisins. Spread in a buttered and floured 8x8-inch or 9x9-inch pan and bake at 350°F for 25 to 30 minutes. Center will NOT test done. Serve with dusted powdered sugar or vanilla ice cream.

Gingerbread Muffins with Lemon Glaze

16 Muffins

2³/₄ cups flour

2¹/₂ teaspoons baking soda

I tablespoon plus ¹/₂ teaspoon ground ginger

I teaspoon ground cinnamon

¹/₈ teaspoon ground cloves

¹/₂ teaspoon salt

¹/₂ cup (I stick) butter at room temperature

¹/₂ cup plus 2 tablespoons sugar

2 large eggs

³/₄ cup molasses

I¹/₃ cups cold water

LEMON GLAZE

I³/₄ cups powdered sugar

5 tablespoons fresh lemon juice

Preheat oven to 350°F. Lightly butter 16 standard muffin cups. Whisk flour, baking soda, ginger, cinnamon, cloves and salt in a medium bowl. Using an electric mixer, beat butter and sugar in large bowl to blend. Add eggs, blend. Beat in molasses. Add ½ dry ingredients, beat until blended. Add the rest of dry ingredients. Gradually add cold water and beat until incorporated. Divide among the muffin cups. Bake 25 minutes, or until pick comes out clean. Spoon 1 teaspoon "whisked" lemon glaze over warm muffins.

We always serve this after family lobster bakes. Ginger helps to settle the tummy!

Recipe Notes

Apple or Blueberry Crisp Pie

Serves 8

Crisps are great, but need a crust to hold them. Pies are great, but the top crust can sometimes be too much. This pie with the crisp topping is the best of both worlds! You may extend your blueberries by adding fresh raspberries, gooseberries... experiment! Another pretty combination is peach and blueberry!

5-6 Granny Smith apples, peeled and sliced OR 2 pints fresh blueberries

1 prepared 9-inch pie crust, unbaked

³/₄ cup flour

1 cup sugar

¹/₃ cup butter, softened

Freshly grated nutmeg

Cinnamon

Dash of salt (when using apples)

Preheat oven to 350°F. Mix flour and sugar and blend in the softened butter. Set aside. Place fruit of choice in prepared pie crust. Grate nutmeg and sprinkle cinnamon over top. If using apples add a dash of salt as well. Cover with flour and sugar mixture. Bake for 40 to 45 minutes, until knife goes easily into fruit when tested. Serve warm with vanilla ice cream.